Amazon 1

MW00799323

Amazon Parrots Pets

Amazon Parrot Essential Owners Guide

by

Martin Barlow

ALL RIGHTS RESERVED. This book contains material protected under International and Federal Copyright Laws and Treaties.

Any unauthorized reprint or use of this material is strictly prohibited. No part of this book may be reproduced or transmitted in any form or by any means, electronic, mechanical or otherwise, including photocopying or recording, or by any information storage and retrieval system without express written permission from the author.

Copyright © 2018

Published by: Zoodoo Publishing

Table of Contents

Introduction

A beautiful parrot with a larger than life personality. This is the perfect description of the Amazon parrot. These birds are multi-colored and incredibly pleasing to the eye. The beauty of the birds is one of the biggest reasons for their popularity as pets.

In addition to that, these birds are extremely intelligent and make great pets. However, they are ideal for those who have some experience with raising parrots. They can be quite a handful. But, when you have got the hang of taking care of these birds, they make great companions for the rest of your life.

Amazon parrots are outgoing, friendly and quite comical. You can spend all day watching them play and climb the perches or the bars of the cage. They simply love to eat, which makes it a lot of fun to try new varieties of food with these birds. Amazon parrots are every parrot lover's dream because they are great talkers. They can pick up several words and even learn to mimic sounds. In any case, these birds are vocal and very talkative. That means you have a great pet to come home to and have long conversations with.

That said, Amazon parrots are demanding birds. They need a lot of attention from their owners. These birds, as mentioned before, are very intelligent. Mental stimulation is just as important for them as a good diet or sanitary living conditions. Without this, these birds tend to develop several behavioral issues. They can get nippy and even aggressive. They tend to scream for attention when they do not get any.

Having a lot of information about parrots is mandatory when you decide to bring home an Amazon parrot. These birds are also exotic which means that they need an exclusive diet and require certain living conditions.

If you are planning to bring an Amazon parrot home, then this book is perfect for you. It covers everything that you need to know from introducing the bird to your home, the food that you should ideally give your pet, the right way to keep them mentally stimulated and the health issues that you should be careful about.

This book is a step-by-step guide to beginners and even with those who are looking for specific information about these birds. It contains practical advice from parrot owners who have raised healthy and happy Amazon parrots.

These birds are a big responsibility and are not for everyone. You need to keep your own lifestyle, your family and other parameters in mind when you are planning to bring one of these birds home. It is a lifelong commitment as some of these birds may live up to 50 years of age. On average, these birds have a life of 30 years.

This book is an attempt to prepare you for an amazing journey that you can have with your parrot. Keeping your parrot happy just requires some effort from your end and this book will tell you how.

Chapter 1: Introduction to Amazon Parrots

Amazon parrots are among the most popular species of parrots kept as pets. These birds belong to the genus *Amazona* which mostly comprises of New World Parrots.

New World parrots are those that originate in the continent of South America. These birds are known for their colorful plumes and their high intelligence. Amazon parrots are also among the largest birds to be bred in captivity and to be kept as pets.

The origin and the natural behavior of any species is important to know before you bring one home as a pet. It lets you know what to expect from the bird and also helps you understand aspects of care such as diet, housing and mating behavior.

This chapter gives you all the details that you need about the history and origins of the magnificent Amazon Parrot.

1. Physical traits of Amazon Parrots

Amazon parrots are among the larger species of parrots, often growing from about 12 to 15 inches in length. These birds are known for their stocky body which makes them look much larger visually. In the wild, most Amazon parrots have green plumes. However, interbreeding and hybrids have led to several varieties that are magnificently colored. The colors usually differ in terms of the markings on the tail, the head and the wings of the bird. Unlike most New World parrots, the Amazon Parrots have tails that are rounded and short.

A characteristic ring is seen around the eyes of the bird. The eyes are beady and small. There is no feathering around the nostrils of the birds most often although some sub-species may have tiny tufts of hair in this area. With each species, the beak coloration is different. The colors range from a light flesh colored beak to dark, black ones. These birds have sharp beaks that need to be trimmed in order to avoid any injuries or accidents. The beak is used for several activities such as holding and climbing.

2. Origins of the Amazon Parrot

Amazon parrots have a wide natural range. They are mostly found in South America and parts of Central America. They are native to the neo-tropic regions. They are also found in the tropical and subtropical regions of West Indies as well.

Although the birds are named after the Amazon River in South Africa, their habitat is quite diverse. These birds are found in wooded forests, the savannahs, tropical forests and even some mountain ranges.

These birds were spotted for the first time by Portuguese sailors. Back then, the birds were named Kriken. This name signified the characteristic screeching noises made by these birds. It is derived from the French word *Criquer* which means screeching. As this name suggests, you can expect your Amazon parrot to be quite the noisemaker.

Since the time these birds were discovered, they were taken to different parts of the world as prized possessions because of their magnificent plumes. The name Amazon Parrot wasn't given to them until the 1800s. This name was used for the first time by Dr.Karl Russ in his scientific journal, "The Speaking Parrot". This is where the bird was descried as a species of parrot with green plumes and a short tail.

After their discovery, these birds were taken in large numbers to Spain from South and Central America. This is when their popularity across Europe grew tremendously. One of the most notable imports of these birds was made by Christopher Colombus. He presented his patron, Queen Isabella of Spain, with two beautiful Cuban Amazon Parrots when he returned from America.

Around the 19th century, the interest in these birds grew among naturalists in Europe. As a result, several studies were conducted about Amazon Parrots and the awareness about these birds increased as well. This is when the royalty of Europe and Britain also became very interested in these birds. They were raised mostly for their incredible ability to speak.

Amazon Parrots had found several admirers across the world towards the end of the 1800s. By then, a lot of research had been conducted and several books had been written about these birds, too. The only drawback was that these birds had not been classified correctly until then and were often mistaken to be other species of green parrots.

Classification of these birds was harder because the limited availability of specimens. Transporting these birds from America all the way to Europe was no easy task. In fact, the classification of Amazon Parrots from regular green parrots is still hard to make. Only experienced aviculturists can differentiate between these birds.

At the turn of the 20th century, a great deal of information about these birds became available. It was during this time that the cost of transportation dropped quite significantly. As a result, more birds were imported. Of course, this also meant that the popularity of these birds increased, too. They were no longer reserved for royalty and just about everyone from innkeepers to people from the educated class owned an Amazon Parrot. During this time, many New World parrots were imported and made popular in Europe.

The demand for the birds was higher in the United States than Europe. This was primarily because of the proximity of native habitats of the Amazon Parrots to the United States. These birds are found in large numbers in the neighboring country of Mexico. As a result, they were a lot easier to import as well.

The World War had a rather major impact on the popularity of these birds. The interest in these birds saw several ebbs and flows. During that time, there were several disease outbreaks among birds raised in captivity. This, along with difficult transport conditions, saw a large dip in the number of parrots that were kept as pets.

With air transport becoming cheaper after the Second World War, the import of parrots also became easier. They were imported in large numbers during that time. Several other species such as the African Grey also came to the foreground after easier means of transport.

With the increasing popularity of the birds, the need for captive breeding and aviculture of various species of Amazon Parrots also grew. Today, there are many restrictions and bans on import of various species of Neo Tropical Parrots. Since pet trading affected the wild populations of these birds, you can only breed these birds in captivity in most parts of the world today. Amazon parrots continue to be popular pets world over and there are several hybrids that are created regularly as well.

3. Taxonomy of Amazon Parrots

Amazon Parrots belong to the Genus *Amazona*. These birds range from medium to large in size as per the species. They have a stocky body that is covered mostly with green plumes. They have a characteristic boxy and round tail. There are various species that differ in the coloration, allowing you to distinguish between them. There are several species such as lilac, red, blue and yellow that will be discussed in the following section.

The first ever scientific description of these birds was made in the 1830s by naturalist, Rene Lesson. Following these, many more naturalists described various species in detail. In order to gain credits for the description of these birds, these naturalists also began to classify the birds hastily. As a result, most of the classification of Amazon Parrots was based on poor evidence and a lack of appropriate specimens. As a result, classification of these birds was heavily debated.

There are better reviews of these birds available today and the classification has been heavily modified. In the year 1991, the Nomenclature of American Ornithologists Union and the Committee of Classification suggested the reclassification of the group *ochrocephala*. This was when the yellow crowned Amazon Parrot was first classified under it. This classification included species like the Yellow Headed Parrot and the Yellow Naped Parrot.

Today, the IUCN Red List of Threatened Species lists over 31 species of Amazon Parrots. Of these, six are classified as endangered. Four have been classified as Close to extinction. This threat to the wild populations has led to several laws and rules being laid down with respect to the import of these birds. Some species have been completely banned from import or export.

The popularity of these birds is one of the primary reasons for the threat faced by them. There are several legal aspects, therefore, that you need to consider before bringing an Amazon Parrot home.

4. Conservation Status of Amazon Parrots

One of the most lucrative businesses in the world is parrot trade. These exotic birds are captured and sold for heavy process. The result of this is that the wild populations of these species began to drop significantly. The natural environment and habitat of the bird was also compromised leading to a population drop. However, even today, these birds are sold illegally. This is why new pet owners should be wary of the sources that they get their birds from.

Between the 1970s and the 1980s, the United States became one of the largest importers of various parrot species. These birds were brought in from across the globe. The number of smuggled birds rose to almost 150,000 per year during this time.

In order to ban illegal trade of exotic species, the Wildlife Conservation Act came into force in the year 1992. As per this act, birds can only be imported for research and other sustainable purposes. With the enforcement of this law, the number of illegal parrots brought in to the United States came down to a few hundred each year. However, illegal trade still persists with Mexico, accounting for the largest number of birds sent to the USA.

In this region, the Defenders of Wildlife works actively to prevent parrot trade. Each year close to 75,000 birds are captured only for illegal pet trade. These numbers led to the formation of the Convention on International Trade which is responsible for protecting Amazon Parrots from being sold in the international pet trade market.

In Europe, a large number of birds contracted the H5N1 flu. This led to the participation of the European Union in the ban on the import of these birds temporarily. The ban became permanent in the year 2007. There are only some countries in Europe where parrot trade is allowed today.

Unfortunately, parrot trade continues in most parts of the world as it is not a high risk offence. The rewards of capturing and smuggling these birds is very high which encourages poaching of these birds.

There isn't enough information available with respect to the number of birds that are actually captured each year. There aren't ample records about the different species of parrots in the world either.

The only report available about parrot trade in Mexico was made as far back as 2006 by Cantu. This is an inadequate report as it only contains information based on interviews conducted with bird traders and union leaders. There is no concrete evidence to suggest the exact number of birds that are traded each year.

Organizations that work towards banning parrot trade do not have enough financial support either. This limits their ability to conduct research and find sustainable solutions to the act of parrot trade.

In 2011, Pires and Moreto suggested some alternative solutions such as installation of CCTV cameras and monitoring of the birds during the mating season. This is a step towards prevention of the crime. The other suggestion was to include parrots as culturally significant symbols in Mexico. The urban population, however, showed very little interest in this solution, making it a hard one to actually implement.

Eco tourism has been suggested as one of the most suitable solutions to the prying issue of parrot trade. This involves the locals joining hands with the government to increase the number of tourists who visit different areas that have large populations of these beautiful species. This activity may also deter the activity of poachers. With tourism becoming more lucrative, poachers may even consider it an alternative to pet trade.

Habitat loss is another significant cause for the depletion of wild populations of Amazon Parrots. In fact, in many areas these birds are considered pests. Since these birds damage agricultural produce such as maize, these birds are trapped and killed as well.

With parrots becoming more endangered each day, it is the responsibility of anyone who wants to own a bird to make sure that they check their sources properly. If you have any doubts about the birds being traded illegally, it is important to report these activities. You can file a report on the official website of the Wildlife Conservation Act and CITES.

5. Different species of Amazon Parrots
There have been various species and hybrids of Amazon Parrots that have been created since they began to be bred in captivity. Some of these birds are also found in the wild. Although there are over 31 species of these birds, some of them have become more popular choices for pets. These species include:

- **Double Yellow Headed Amazon**
  Scientific name: *Amazona oratrix*
  Also known as the Yellow Headed Parrot or the Yellow Headed Amazon, these birds are popular because of their ability to speak. They are the best among all the other species when it comes to picking up human vocabulary.

  These birds are native to the coast of Mexico and Central America. The distinct yellow forehead lends them the name. The rest of the body is green. These birds are curious and very active. Their queer body language including dilating their pupils quickly and tilting the head almost upside down makes them even more popular choices as pets.

- **Blue Fronted Amazons**
  Scientific name: *Amazona aestiva*
  These birds have a patch of blue feathers just above the beak and hence get this name. These feathers blend into shades of yellow and white before merging into the green plumes on the body. The shade of the blue feathers on the head varies from violet blue to turquoise as per the sub species.

  These birds require a lot of attention and need to stick to a routine when it comes to feeding time or even playtime. These birds are also known to sing and mimic quite well.

- **Green Cheeked Amazons**
  Scientific name: *Amazona viridigenalis*
  They are amongst the most attractive of all Amazon Parrots. The feathers are a darker green in color while the under feathers are a pale green color. The cheeks have a patch of iridescent green feathers that have a lilac or purple ring around them.

  These birds are known for their extremely pleasant demeanor. They love to play, which makes them a popular choice as pets. They are also known to be great companions who love to spend a lot of time with their owners.

- **Lilac Crowned Amazons**
  Scientific name: *Amazona finschi*
  These birds were first documented in the late 1800s by Dr.Otto Finsch. He described them in great detail in his journals. The name comes from the lilac feathers on the crown of the bird's head. The forehead and the lores have beautiful red feathers. The lilac coloration goes down to the neck of the bird and even make a ring around the cheeks of the bird.

  These birds are native to the Pacific slopes in the Western part of Mexico. They are known to be highly energetic birds.

- **Mealy Amazona**
  Scientific name: *Amazona farinose*

These birds are also called the Blue Crowned Mealy or the Mealy Parrot. They are the largest of all Amazon Parrots, often growing up to 16 inches in length as adults. The green and grey coloration of the bird makes it look like it has a coating of flour on its body. That is why the name, Mealy Amazon. The tail of the birds has a very distinct blue tip and the crown has bright blue feathers.

These birds are commonly found in Bolivia, Eastern parts of Brazil and Southern Mexico.

- **Orange Winged Amazon**
  Scientific name: *Amazonan Amazonica*
  Like most Amazon Parrots, these birds have a green body, too. Their distinct feature is the bright orange and blue coloration that is seen on the face and head. They also have bright orange feathers that lend them the name. These colors are seen only after the bird is fully mature.

  These birds are native to the central and northern parts of South America and a few populations are also seen in Trinidad and Tobago.

- **Panaman Amazon**
  Scientific name: *Amazona panamensis*
  These birds rose to popularity only a few decades ago. They are also called the Panama Yellow Fronted Amazon. They are quite similar to the Yellow Crowned Amazon Parrots in appearance. What distinguishes them from the species is that the feathers are darker and their structure is smaller.

  These birds are native to the western part of Panama. They are also found in the Pearl islands, Coiba and Colombia. These birds are extremely intelligent and curious and are known for being good talkers.

- **Red Lored Amazon**
  Scientific name: *Amazona autunmalis*
  The face of these birds is extremely colorful. They also go by the name of Yellow Cheeked Amazons. The beautiful face of the bird has made them popular among bird lovers. The lores are bright red in color and the cheeks are a contrasting bright yellow.

These birds are also great pets as they are very friendly. They are native to Eastern Mexico and Central America. A few populations are also found in Belize, Honduras and Guatemala.

- **White Fronted Amazon**
  Scientific name: *Amazona abiforns*
  They are the smallest of all Amazon Parrots. These birds are very big in terms of their personality. They love to play and are great talkers. They are curious and bold birds. They are one of the two Amazon species where you can tell the male apart from the female. This means that they are sexually dimorphic. The forehead of the bird has a yellowish or whitish coloration.

  They are native to Central America with several populations also found in Nicarhua, Belize, Costa Rica, El Salvador and Puerto Rico.

- **Yellow Crowned Amazon**
  Scientific name: *Amazona ochrocephala*
  These birds are mostly green in color like most Amazon Parrots. What sets them apart is the yellow coloration on the forehead. They are different from the double yellow headed Amazons, as the yellow coloration does not extend to the neck and the whole head. Sometimes, they are also referred to as the Single Yellow Headed Amazons. The head of these birds are also more rounded in comparison to the Double Yellow Headed Amazon.

  They are extremely affectionate birds and are quite smart too. They are good talkers. Most populations of these birds are seen in the Central region of America. There are some populations in Peru, Trinidad and the South of the Amazon Basin.

- **Yellow Naped Amazon**
  Scientific name: *Amazona auropalliata*
  Another common name for these birds is the Golden Naped Amazons. They have a patch of light yellow feathers on the nape of the neck. Other than that, they are covered with green plumes on their body.

  These birds are known to be a lot more obedient in comparison to other species of Amazon Parrots. They are extremely confident birds but are easier to train. They are hardy birds that do well indoors and in outdoor aviaries. They are native to El Salvador, Mexico, Guatemala and the Honduras.

Irrespective of the species of Amazon Parrots that you bring home, the care and the requirements remain the same. They have almost similar requirements in terms of food, housing and healthcare.

Chapter 2: Things to Know About Amazon Parrots

Before you bring an Amazon Parrot home, there are a few things that you need to make note of. These exotic, protected species are quite different from other popular species of parrots that are kept as pets.

Not only do you have to make sure that you understand their behavior, you also need to be sure that you are bringing a parrot home legally. Here are some of the most important things that you need to know before you actually bring one of these birds home.

1. Natural behavior of the birds

A major part of a bird's natural instincts and behavior is retained even when it is bred in captivity. While the birds can be hand-tamed and trained, there are some traits in their personality that are ingrained in their DNA.

Learning about this natural behavior will help you understand your bird better. The result of this is that you will be able to provide for your bird better and keep him happier.

- **These birds are diurnal:** This means that the birds are active during the day. Therefore, the first meal of the bird should be given to them early in the morning. In the wild, the birds leave the nest before sunrise in order to find food. They return to their roosting spots at dusk and will rest there. This is common to all Amazon Parrots except for the Pantagonian Amazon Parrot which is nocturnal. These birds are excessively active on full moon days.

- **The habitats of the bird are diverse:** You will find Amazon Parrots in a range of habitats including open savannahs and rain forests. This makes the birds hardy pets that can adjust to indoors and outdoors alike. Sometimes, the birds are also seen on limestone cliffs in mountainous areas.

- **They are very resilient:** Be it physically or emotionally, Amazon Parrots are known to be very resilient. They are birds with a very strong personality and even tend to do just as they please at times. These birds also have a range of different temperaments. From being mild and timid, these birds can even be phobic and aggressive at times. Birds that share an aviary with other species such as African Greys

16

tend to be scared easily. They can develop this behavior even when they are unwell. However, in most cases the birds are curious and bold. Any sudden change in the nature of the bird is an indication that he or she may be unwell. In case of many severe health issues such as Psittacine Beak and Feather Disorder, the first thing that you notice is that the bird becomes unreasonably fearful and phobic.

- **They develop behavioral issues:** With birds as intelligent as the Amazon Parrots, keeping an eye on their behavior is a must. If not, they may develop issues such as biting or screaming. You should make sure that you give your bird some basic training. They should also be given proper care and a lot of good food and exercise in order to keep them from developing these issues. Birds that undergo any trauma or ones that face neglect from their owners will display extreme behavioral issues as a means to get the attention that they need. This includes issues like feather plucking as well. Of course, feather plucking is also an indication of health issues. It is also common in these birds when they hit puberty. You can consult the vet if these issues develop all of a sudden. Change in the diet or better hygiene could be easy solutions to this problem.

- **They are social birds:** Amazon Parrots live in large flocks in the wild. They are very social and can even thrive with flocks of other species of birds. These birds can become aggressive as a flock if they see any threat to their food or well-being, however. They display aggression through their body language in most cases. They tend to puff their feathers up as a sign of threat. This means that you need to back off immediately unless you want to be attacked. Never pick up a bird with puffed up feathers. In most cases, these birds love their flocks and are very gentle with the members of the flock. It also means that you need to spend some time with your bird to build that trust and bond.

- **These birds are loud:** As mentioned before, Amazon Parrots are known for their characteristic screech. This screech is a way of communicating with the mates in the wild in most cases. When they separate from each other while they are out looking for food, Amazon Parrots let out a distinct screech to look for their mates. The screech is also a sign of distress or an attempt to scare someone away. Sometimes, the birds also scream for attention. There are tips to deal with this in the following chapters. Letting your bird scream and then doing what they want you to will become a way for the bird to manipulate you. Spending more time with the bird and keeping them physically and mentally stimulated can curb the screaming.

Remember that each bird comes with a distinct personality. So, there could be several interesting traits and challenges that you will come across with your own pet. Making sure that they get the right care and attention is the easiest way to manage the behavior of your Amazon Parrot. Correct introductions to the new home and the members of your home also matter quite a bit. We will discuss all of these in detail in the next chapter.

2. Legal considerations

Since Amazon Parrots are exotic birds, there are several legal aspects to keeping one in your home. There are some rules that even apply to keeping and breeding these birds in captivity. Here are some legal considerations that you need to make when you bring home an Amazon Parrot:

Get the necessary license

In certain countries, getting a license to own a parrot is mandatory. To learn more about parrot licenses, get in touch with the local wildlife authorities in your city. You will have to fulfill some requirements in order to get a valid license.

In Australia, for instance, bird owners have to get a license. The license can be obtained from the office of Environment and Heritage. They also monitor the species that you bring home on a regular basis. In Australia, bird owners can get two classes of licenses- Class 1 and Class 2. Class 1 license is meant for keeping birds that are native to the region that you live in. These birds are a lot easier to care for.

The Class 2 license is meant for those who want to bring home exotic birds that have specific care requirements. You can only get this license if you are over 16 years of age. Birds that are kept without the necessary license can be seized and taken away.

Check your rental agreement or lease

Sometimes, the rental agreement or lease may contain a "no pets" clause. If you bring the bird home despite this, it may create several legal issues. You can even get evicted from your home for not abiding by this clause. Usually those who keep pets when they are bound by a no pet's clause will receive a month's notice to vacate your home.

There is a three month clause attached to this clause at times. This means that if you have had a pet for three months or more despite the "no pets" agreement, the rule cannot be enforced by the owner if he failed to notice the bird in this period.

A simpler way is to inform your landlord about your desire to have a parrot as a pet. These laws may be specific to animals like dogs and cats. You may also have to ensure your landlord that the bird will not be a nuisance to neighbors in terms of making noise or messing up the premises.

Take permission from neighbors

Remember that Amazon Parrots can be very noisy. They screech quite loudly and if not trained properly, this behavior may be executed all day long. In this case, the neighbors have every right to object to you having the bird at home. You may even find yourself in the midst of legal issues if you do not pay heed to these complaints. There are several legal cases each year that are related to pets. While most are related to dogs or larger animals, there are some specific to birds as well.

Poorly trained birds are also a threat to other pets or children. If your bird does have an accident with someone visiting your home, you can be sued. This will mean that you will have to compensate for the damage and even reimburse medical bills, if any.

Limitations in the number of pets you can keep

There are certain zoning laws in some cities and states that put a limit on the number of birds that each home can have. This law usually applies when you keep your birds in outdoor aviaries. In any case, checking with the local wildlife authorities is a good idea, especially if you want to keep your bird outdoors.

These rules are also applicable to breeders. If you have an aviary illegally, you can be fined heavily. You will also lose the aviary and the birds. If the birds are poorly maintained and are causing any nuisance, you will be penalized heavily.

The number of birds per household is normally restricted to five. There are lots of factors that determine this number, including the availability of space and the consent of the neighbors.

The laws are specific to each country and state. As a result, they may vary significantly. Rules can even extend to pet burial and most state that you cannot bury a pet in city limits. You need be aware of all these rules before you bring your bird home.

3. Can you manage an Amazon Parrot

The most important thing that you need to ask yourself is if you can manage the responsibility of an Amazon Parrot. These birds are not just about a pretty bird in a cage. They are very intelligent and need a lot of attention and care from your end. You also need to manage your schedule as per the bird. Here are some things that you should know about having an Amazon Parrot as a pet to understand the responsibility:

- **They demand time:** As mentioned before, these birds are very social and intelligent. They thrive best when they are interacting with their flock members. You need to train your bird and keep him entertained in order to ensure that he is healthy and to prevent behavior issues.

  Even with the largest and most spacious cage filled with accessories, you need to do your bit to keep the bird entertained. You have to give your bird time outside the cage so that they can form a strong bond with you and your family.

  Make sure that all the members of your family spend ample time with the bird. This helps everyone understand the behavior and also have positive interactions with him. The more you observe, the more you will be able to determine any change in your bird's behavior. This can be extremely useful to determine any illness in your bird in the future.

- **They get quite messy:** You will need to clean up after your parrot. They poop all the time and are even messy eaters. They will also shed feathers. They do so in large quantities, especially during the molting season. You need to make sure that the cage and the food and water bowls are extremely clean to prevent any infections.

  Even when your bird is potty trained, there could be accidents in the house that you need to take care of. Since the metabolism of the birds is so high, this is an issue that may become irksome to you.

- **The purpose of bringing the parrot home:** You must know why you are bringing the bird home before you do. If you are only going by appearances, then you may want to learn a little more and spend some time with these birds before you take on the responsibility. They need constant care and can make great companions provided you are ready for them.

If the bird is being chosen as a companion for your child, you may want to reconsider it. Amazon Parrots are large birds and if they are startled or scared, they can inflict serious injuries. Children below the age of 16 years should receive assistance with the bird. This means that you need to take care of activities like grooming and training the birds and leave simpler responsibilities like entertaining the bird to the child.

4. Cost of raising an Amazon Parrot

After all these considerations, the most important one is whether you can afford the bird or not. Amazon Parrots are a long term investment as they live up to 35 years of age. You should bring the bird home only if you can sustain the following expenses for that much time:

One time investment:
- Cost of the bird: $750-$1500 or £300-800
- Cage and housing- $400-$1000

Recurring costs:
- Food :$30 -60 or £15-25 per month
- Toys; $20-40 04 £8-20 per month
- Veterinary care: $50-75 per visit.

This adds up to an initial investment up to $1800 or £750. The recurring costs add up to almost $200 or £150 with any miscellaneous costs. Make sure that you have this monthly budget. You can even start by putting this amount away for a few months before you bring the parrot home to see if you can really afford it.

Chapter 3: Finding the Right Sources

There are two things to finding the right source to get your bird from. First, the bird should be healthy. Second, the bird should be bred legally. You have several options and here are some tips to find the best among them.

1. Buying from breeders

The best source for an Amazon Parrot would be a reliable breeder. They are equipped with a lot of information about the species. In addition to that, the genuine breeders thrive to keep the birds healthy and happy. They practice ethical breeding techniques that make sure that you get a bird with good genes into your home. Here are some tips to find the right breeder.

Things to consider

There are three important aspects to buying from a breeder:

Are the birds bred properly?

If you notice that the conditions that the birds are kept in are not sanitary, then there is a good chance that there are several communicable diseases within the flock. Even diseases like proventricular dilation could exist. This makes the birds depressed and will also lead to rapid weight loss. The risk is higher with diseases like Chlamydiosis and Salmonellosis that can be contracted by humans as well. In addition to that, having a sick bird at home can be difficult and extremely expensive.

Is the bird smuggled?

This is very important, especially with Amazon Parrots. First, smuggling birds is illegal. Second, when the birds are smuggled they are treated very badly. They are transported in the air vents of vehicles and in other small and congested places. These birds are simply treated as commodities. Buying a bird from such a breeder also means that you are buying into the illegal pet trade.

Has the breeder ever given birds away?

This may be a sign that the breeder is inexperienced. Every year several birds are abandoned and sent away into shelters. This is primarily because they become too difficult for breeders and even some pet owners to deal with.

There are laws related to the abandonment of birds to ensure that they are never left in the lurch. In case of birds that have been bred in captivity, they can be in great danger when they are left out into the wild by breeders who cannot care for them. They can be attacked by predators or even other flocks of birds. These attacks can also be fatal at times.

How to find a genuine breeder

The first step to bringing home an Amazon Parrot is to find the perfect breeder. Here are a few tips that will be of great assistance:

- Look for a local breeder who works in an area that is conveniently located from your home.

- You can get a list of breeders on the Internet. You can even look for advertisements about birds for sale in the classifieds section of your local newspaper.

- When you find a listing that seems genuine, you can contact them.

- The Internet, however is your best bet. You can find several breeder directories that will list out the options available in your city and in your locality.

- Look for details of local bird groups and clubs online. You will also be able to meet several other Amazon Parrot owners in these clubs who can be very valuable in providing you with information and assistance with your pet.

- Ask for recommendations from Amazon Parrot owners or from people who own parrots. You can get a firsthand account from them about their experiences with various breeders.

  - You can even look for clubs that work towards the protection and conservation of exotic birds. These clubs are extremely passionate about learning about Amazon Parrots and other exotic birds. They also take great responsibility in ensuring that the birds are bred correctly. These clubs will only connect you with the best and most reliable breeders in your city. They may even help you raise your Amazon Parrot properly.

Once you have found a breeder who looks promising, make sure you visit their facility. Although several breeders have websites and an active online presence, remember that seeing is believing. When you visit the facility, you will get a good idea about the breeding practices and the intentions of the breeder.

The first interview with your breeder is crucial to understanding whether or not he is the right person to buy your Amazon parrot from. You can ask the breeder the following questions to get a good idea about their husbandry methods and breeding practices:

- How much experience do they have with breeding and raising Amazon Parrots?
- Are the birds hand reared?
- What are the birds fed?
- How often are the birds bred each year?
- Do they have an avian vet whom they can recommend?

A genuine breeder will be interested to answer any question that you have. These breeders genuinely care about their birds. They will be able to provide you with answers instantly and confidently.

A good breeder takes great pride in his facility. He will want to show you how the birds are raised and will know a lot about each bird that you are shown. The enthusiasm of the breeder is a great quality to look for.

As you converse with the breeder, you will get a fair idea of the interest of the breeder. A good breeder will be eager to share every bit of information that he has about Amazon Parrots. On the other hand, if the breeder is making excuses to show you the aviary or the other areas at the facility, it is a red flag.

If you notice any hesitation in providing answers to your questions, it means that the breeder is most likely looking at the commercial interest in breeding and raising Amazon Parrots. The breeders should be eager to tell you more about the bird. However, if his only point of interest is making a sale, then look for more options.

The breeder that you choose is not only crucial for you to obtain birds that are healthy. The breeder can also become a great source of information when you face any challenges when it comes to raising your beloved pet.

The next thing you need to make sure is that you check the facility thoroughly before you buy a bird. The best kind of aviary is a closed one. Here, quarantining and sanitation is of utmost importance.

When you are going around the facility and taking a look around, there are some things that you need to keep an eye on:

- Make sure the cages are clean. There should not be any feces on the floor or in the food bowl. The floor and the food bowls should be free from feathers and feather dust to a good extent. In general, the cage should not look unkempt. Any good breeder will make sure that the birds are kept in a healthy and clean environment. This is a sign that the birds are at a lesser risk of diseases and infections.

- The food should be of good quality. Make sure that the birds are not restricted to a seed or pellet diet. For Amazon Parrots, having a large variety of foods is a must. A peek into the food bowl should reveal some fresh produce as well. If not, you will have to first introduce the bird to a good diet once you bring him or her home. That can be a challenge.

- The appearance of the birds also plays a very important role. Normally, like any other parrot, Amazon Parrots are very alert and curious. If the bird stays on the floor of the cage or seems to back away into a corner when you approach him, it is a sign that he is not comfortable being around people. This may imply that he is not hand raised. In addition to that, the bird may also have health issues. Buying birds that are not friendly or are seemingly sick is certainly not a good idea. This is a sign that you have to look for other options.

When you have found a breeder who makes you comfortable enough to make a purchase, you can negotiate the sales terms. If the bird is still being hand trained or if the breeder has some special conditions for the purchase, you will not be able to take the bird home immediately. Some breeders insist that you spend some time with the bird before you take him home.

When you are waiting for the breeder to give you a clearance to take the bird home, you can make all the necessary preparations. This means you will have enough time to set up the cage of the bird, buy the toys, stick up on food and also get your family prepared. If you have everything ready for the bird to move in, then you will reduce a lot of stress on the part of the bird.

2. Buying from pet stores

There are a few red flags which show that a certain pet store may either be involved in some illegal trade of birds or that they simply treat these birds as commercial commodities.

If you see any of the following practices with respect to the Amazon Parrots, you need to choose a different source. You can also report these practices to the Forest Authority or any Animal Welfare authority as they are signs that the source is involved in illegal practices of pet trade:

- The bird is carried upside down or the feet are tied when he is being transported.

- The birds are not placed in accordance to the species. Every specie should be kept separately with the right labels outside the display area.

- Any band that is being used to identify the bird is not placed correctly and is causing trauma.

- Predator species are not kept far apart from the birds. This may lead to behavioral issues in the bird that you will have to deal with later on.

Choosing a good pet store

Pet stores are a lot more convenient as you will find several of them close to your home. But you need to understand that Amazon Parrots are exotic species and not every pet store is able to provide good care for these birds. You need to make sure that you are bringing home a healthy and happy bird. For this, the pet store that you choose should be able to give you a good quality bird. Here are a few tips to select a good pet store:

- **Cleanliness:** The pet store should not have an unpleasant odor when you walk in. Of course, you will be able to smell the fur and feathers but if you want to close your nose as soon as you enter, it means that the animals have not been maintained properly. The cages should not be jammed closed to one another. They should be arranged in such a way that you can navigate through the store and look at the animals that have been kept there for sale.

- **The Animals and Birds:** If you find painted or dyed fish in the store, it is a commercial space that you want to run from. Also, it is very unusual for a pet store to have birds and reptiles together. This is because each of them requires a lot of care individually. Unless you have enough employees to take care of these creatures, it is impossible to provide good care. So if your pet store sells an Amazon Parrot and a reptile, you must make sure that you ask them how they manage to take care both creatures efficiently.

- **Willingness to help:** The staff at the pet store should be willing to help you look around and choose a bird for yourself. They should be able to answer your queries clearly and should not beat around the bush. Also, observe the way they talk about the animals in their store. If they are belittling another bird or animal because it is less expensive than your Amazon Parrot, they are only trying to make a sale. They should also be able to handle the birds easily and should be gentle while doing so. This shows that they spend time with the animals and interact with them.

- **Will provide health guarantee:** A pet store that provides a health guarantee is definitely the best. They are absolutely sure about the quality of animals and birds in their store and will, therefore, give you a written guarantee. The duration of this guarantee is usually shorter than the one you can get from a breeder. You must certainly ask for a guarantee or contract when you are having the birds shipped.

You can also ask them about how they quarantine birds and how they handle birds from different sources. If this is a regular practice, it means that your birds are most likely going to be healthy.

3. Getting a health guarantee

Whether you are buying from a breeder or a pet store, a health guarantee is a must. With birds, it is always reasonable to believe that the bird may not be in the best of his health when you make a purchase. Should you have to return the bird, a health guarantee ensures that you get a full refund. It is best that you avoid breeders who do not provide a health guarantee.

Without a health guarantee, it is almost impossible for a buyer to prove that the breeder knew about the illness when he made a sale. With a written health guarantee, you can make up for this lack of legal protection on part of the buyer.

A health guarantee works both ways. It protects a seller if the new owner is negligent. It also helps the buyer in case the breeder did not disclose any disease that the bird could be carrying. There are a few conditions that every health guarantee contains:

- The health of your bird is guaranteed for a total of three days as long as the bird has been thoroughly examined by a certified Avian Vet. This is an expense that you need to take care of.

  Should the veterinary find any issues that makes the health of the bird unsatisfactory, you need written documentation that will state the issues.

  You must return the bird immediately for a full refund. The species and the band number of the bird must be mentioned in the document provided. The breeder will not reimburse the vet fees or any expense that you have to bear for transportation.

- In case the bird dies within 12 days of purchase, you need to make sure that a necropsy is conducted within 72 hours after the death of the bird. If you are not able to conduct the necropsy immediately, the body must be refrigerated until the tests are conducted.

  The reports of the necropsy should be sent to the veterinarian of the breeder and must include the species and the band number. If these reports prove beyond any doubt that the bird had any health issues that originated before the purchase, you will be able to get a full reimbursement or a replacement.

  Some breeders will also allow you a 6 month window during which a death of the bird will ensure reimbursement, provided a proper necropsy is conducted.

  The breeder will not be held responsible for any expenses that you have to bear for these tests. You will also not hold the breeder liable if any bird from your existing flock develops any problem. It is mandatory to quarantine every new bird and if you do not do so, you cannot hold the breeder responsible.

- You must ensure that the bird has been quarantined adequately when you bring him home. He should be kept away from the other birds for at least 30 days before introducing him into the flock.

- If you already have other birds at home for a year or more, you will have to provide all the medical records of the bird and correct documentation for their health. It is possible that viruses that infect birds stay in a certain environment for many hours even after the bird has recovered fully.

- Negligence on part of the owner does not make the breeder liable for any return or reimbursement. For instance, if you leave the bird in the car on a hot day or if you do not provide the bird with adequate food and care, you cannot hold the breeder responsible for any health issues or even death.

Of course, a health guarantee does not cover for any behavioral or psychological issues. It is your responsibility to make sure that you spend time with the bird to understand his behavior before you make the purchase.

4. Adopting Amazon Parrots

There are many cases where Amazon Parrots are abandoned either because they were too overwhelming for the owners or because they developed some behavioral issues. You have the option of adopting an Amazon Parrot. It is the cheapest option. However, you need to be experienced to bring home an Amazon Parrot from a shelter or a rescue for the following reasons.

- **The bird comes with baggage:** When birds need rehoming, there are chances that the bird has had past experiences that are pleasant or not so pleasant. In any case, the whole process of shifting homes is very traumatic and stressful for birds. When adopting from a reputed rescue center, the staff will be able to give you a brief history of the bird's life and will also tell you how you can deal with the problems that you may encounter. This is a good thing as you will receive enough education about the personality and the specific requirements of a certain bird.

- **Birds can change over time:** When you adopt a baby bird, you may feel like his personality is very mild and friendly. However, there is no guarantee that the personality will remain the same when the bird reaches sexual maturity. Some of them may become aggressive or shy depending upon their individual personality. So, always be prepared. If you are new to the world of parrots, having someone who can help you cope with these issues is a good idea.

- **It is a financial commitment:** Bringing home a bird that is injured or has any history of abuse is a big financial commitment. You will have to make regular visits to the vet to ensure that your bird is in top health at all times. The medicines that you need to buy for your bird are a big investment, too. Only when you are ready to take that on should you adopt a bird.

- **You need to make time:** With a bird who is recovering in your home, you cannot leave him alone all the time. The fact that he was neglected has led to the stress and the health issues in the first place. If the bird has been given up by a loving home because they were unable to care for it, it is even worse as the bird must have created strong bonds already. This is especially true for wonderfully social birds like the Amazon Parrot. If you are busy and do not have the time to bond with your bird and build the required trust, you must definitely not adopt one.

The process of adopting the bird

The first step to adopting an Amazon Parrot is to fill out an application form for adoption. This application form will ask for details about your profession, your experience with birds and also the reason for adoption.

Following this application form, you will be asked to take basics lessons about caring for Amazon Parrots. These lessons could either be online or offline. You will also be given access to a lot of their educational material that you can refer to after taking the bird home. Many adoption agencies require that you complete a certain number of these basics classes before you are allowed to take a bird home.

After you have completed the required number of training hours, you will be allowed to take a tour of the aviary and the adoption center. That way, you get an idea about all the birds that are available for adoption. There are several cases when people decide that they want a certain bird but end up getting a different species altogether.

The idea is to form a bond with the right bird. Amazon Parrots are birds with large personalities. If your personality does not match the bird's personality, you will have a tough time getting your bird to bond with you and actually want to be around you.

The last thing to do would be to visit the bird of your choice frequently. Once you have made up your mind to take a certain Amazon Parrot home, you need to let the bird get acquainted with you. You will also learn simple things like handling the bird, feeding him and cleaning the cage up etc. from the experts at the adoption agency.

Sometimes, it may so happen that you set your heart and mind on one bird who just does not seem to be interested. It is natural for that to happen. All you need to do is be patient with the bird and visit him as many times as you can.

When you are ready to take the bird home, most of these adoption centers will pay a visit to your home and will take care of all the little details required to help you get the bird settled into your home.

Now, if you already have pet birds at home, you will be required to present a full veterinary test result of each bird. This helps the agency ensure that the bird they are sending to your home does not have any vulnerability to fatal diseases. There are certain health standards that each of these agencies set for the health of your pet bird.

Are there any fees involved?
Most agencies and foundations will charge you an application fee that will include access to educational DVDs, toys and other assistance from the foundation.

You will also have to pay an adoption fee that may go up to $100 or £500 for an Amazon Parrot. These two separate fees are charged to make sure that you get all the assistance that you need with respect to making a positive start with your Amazon Parrot.

In addition to that, most agencies charge a rather high fee to ensure that the individuals who are investing in the bird are genuinely interested in having the bird. These fees will ward off people who want to just take the bird home for free with no clue about its care. Of course, you also need to consider the care provided to these birds while they are under the care of the foundation. These fees cover all of that including the medical requirements of your bird. It is also the only source to pay the dedicated staff who take care of these abandoned or rescued bird's day in and day out.

From the time you make the application for an Amazon Parrot, it takes about 6-10 weeks for it to be approved and for the bird to be sent to your home. Most of these centers will also have a probationary period of 90 days during which you will have to keep sending records of how the bird is progressing to them. They will also pay home visits to ensure that the bird is being maintained well without any health issues. If the ambience or the facilities provided to the bird are not good enough, the bird will be taken back with no reimbursement of the adoption fee.

Chapter 4: Preparing for an Amazon Parrot

You need to do a good deal of homework before you bring the Amazon Parrot home. This means preparing yourself and preparing your home for the arrival of the bird.

This chapter will tell you about everything that you will need in order to be fully prepared. This will ensure that from the first day of the bird's arrival in your home, you will have positive interactions.

1. How to get yourself prepared?

There are three simple things that you can do to check if you are prepared for the bird and whether or not the Amazon Parrot is a good pet for your household:

- Foster an Amazon Parrot for a few days. You can volunteer to care for an Amazon Parrot that belongs to a friend or to a relative. You can alternatively spend time at rescue shelters. Taking care of the bird will tell you how hard it can actually get.
- Make sure that you research about the bird in detail. The better you know about a certain species, the better you will be able to provide for it.
- You can even join online forums or local bird clubs to learn about these birds. You will get information from people who have hands on experience with the bird.

Once you have prepared yourself, it is time for you to make sure that the bird has a comfortable home to come into.

2. Preparing the housing area

Don't wait for the bird to come home to set the housing area up. Although you may have a temporary carrier in place when you bring the bird home from the breeder or the pet store, try to move him into the permanent housing area the day you bring him home.

That way, you will give your bird all the time to settle down. Changing cages in the midst of his settling down process adds to the stress that he is already experiencing.

The housing area is where your bird is going to spend most of his time. So, you need to make sure that it is perfect. There are a few things that you need to think about when you set up the housing area:

- The size of the cage
- The material used to build it
- The type of cage
- The placement of the cage
- The accessories that you put into the cage

Cage size

Amazon Parrots are large birds. Nevertheless, they need to have enough space to flap around and even fly a little in the housing area. You need to make sure that the bird is able to spread his wings in all directions when he is in the cage. The minimum size of the cage is 42X42X72 for the bird to feel comfortable in it.

Remember that your bird may spend the whole day in the cage or at least 12 hours every day. So, making sure that the cage is safe is a must.

If you are able to get a cage that is double the recommended size, it is called a true flight cage. This means that the bird is actually able to fly in this cage. You must also be able to fit in perches in the cage without getting in the way of the bird.

If the cage is way too small, there can be unwanted injuries when the bird flaps his wings. The feathers or the wings will get caught in the bars, leading to broken feathers and wings.

Cage material

Amazon Parrots are extremely powerful birds. If you do not get a strong enough cage, it will lead to escapes. The best material for an Amazon Parrot cage is stainless steel. These cages are a lot more expensive than the powder coated ones.

However, the ease with which the birds can bend the bars of any other material makes it worth spending the money. You could consider it a onetime investment. Any other material will be destroyed in just a few weeks of putting the bird in.

With stainless steel you can also avoid the problem of peeling paint. As the birds climb the cage, they may peel the paint off and even ingest it. Even if the paint is said to be lead free, you need to make sure that the flakes or the chunks of paint will not cause any internal damage to the bird. The best thing is to avoid any cage or housing that contains paint.

Cage Style

There are several types of cages that are available to you. Some are ornamental while others are practical. In the case of Amazon Parrots, the best options include the dome top cage and the play top cage. The dome top cage is popular because there is a lot of space available inside for you to add accessories like perches.

In case of the play top cages, you have a flat surface on top that becomes a great playing area for the birds. This gives your bird ample room outdoors to play and have a good time.

When you buy a cage for your Amazon Parrot, you also need to check things like the lock on the doors, the distance between the bars, the thickness of the bars etc. If the cage has horizontal bars, it makes climbing a lot easier. Now, you also need to make sure that the bars have been welded into place to ensure that they are sturdy.

Cage placement

The cage must occupy a quiet area in your home that is free from movements of people. There should be ample, yet not harsh sunlight. The cage that you place the Amazon Parrot in should be away from the main road or noisy streets that may startle the birds. The best place would be one of the rooms in your home where the cage is placed against a wall for the bird to feel comfortable and secure. The bird should be able to watch you from this area but should not be in the middle of your activity.

Cage accessories

It is the accessories that complete the cage set up. If you just have an empty cage, you will not be successful in creating any positive associations that will make the bird want to go back into the cage. You need several accessories like toys and perches that will make the cage a rather interesting place for the bird to be in. This will come in very handy when you begin to train the bird. So, make sure the following accessories are included:

- **Toys:** Toys are the most important accessories to ensure that the bird is mentally stimulated. There are different kinds of toys that you can opt for including climbing toys, chewing toys and foraging toys. Each one offers a different kind of experience for your bird.

  When choosing these toys, make sure that they are free from small parts that could be swallowed by the bird. You also need to make sure

34

that the material used does not consist of any toxins in the paint or the material of construction. Only use good quality toys inside the cage of your bird.

Lastly, when you are hanging the toys, avoid using wires and strings. The bird may get tangled in these wires or threads, leading to cuts and even choking. You will get bird safe hooks with most of the good quality toys. You can also use a safer alternative which is steel chains. These are sturdy and are suitable to even hold up the perch which will carry the entire weight of the large Amazon Parrot. With this bird, you need to be sure that all suspended items are sturdy to prevent falls and injuries.

- **Perches:** A proper perch is a must for your bird to have a good resting area. You can put up store bought perches that are available in several sizes and colors or may even make a perch out of wood yourself. If you are using a twig or piece of wood as the perch, make sure that the material is free from the poop of any wild birds. That way, you can be assured that the bird will not develop infections or other diseases.

For birds, it is very important for them to be able to trust the perching area. If it breaks or if the bird has any accident while on the perch, he will simply never get back on the perch again. That is why you need to make sure that it is hung up with good quality chains or hooks. These chains should be safe and should not have any sharp ends that may hurt the bird.

- **Food and water bowls:** Of course, your cage is incomplete without these two important elements. You need to have food and water bowls that are easy for the bird to eat or drink from. At the same time, they should be free from any toxic elements like lead or zinc.

It is recommended that you use only stainless steel or porcelain bowls for your bird cage. These materials are not damaged easily and are also very easy to clean. Do not buy any bowls with intricate design elements as they will be harder to clean and may have left overs of fruit and vegetables that can make your bird very unwell.

Place these food and water bowls near the door of the cage. This will make it much easier for you to access them. This placement will also be very useful when you are training your bird to go in and out of the cage.

- **The substrate:** Birds are pooping machines. On average, your Amazon Parrot will poop every 15 minutes. Therefore, you need to line the cage with material that is absorbent enough and safe for the bird at the same time.

  The best option is layers of newspaper, although it is debated that the ink in the paper can be hazardous to the bird's health. Choose matte finish papers without too many pictures to address this issue. You must never use wood shavings as the bird may develop several health issues due to damp wood.

  It is a good idea to place a grate on the floor of the cage to make sure that your bird is not walking all over his own poop.

You can add additional elements such as a sleeping tent to make your cage look more attractive. Of course, people like to add colorful toys and ribbons as well to make the cage seem more ornamental. In any case, the simpler the better as your bird will also be safe while the cage is complete with all the basic elements in it. You can get creative and change the interiors from time to time.

3. Bird Proofing

Making your home safe for the bird should be your priority. There are several household items that can pose a threat to your pet bird. Although good training can avoid many accidents, you can never be too sure. Before your bird is brought home, a few mandatory bird proofing measures must be taken.

- Make sure that the cage is not placed on a hard surface. Should your bird have a fall, he can sustain serious injuries.

- The windows should be marked or should have a safe object hanging in front of it. That way, you will not have any instance of the bird flying into the windows and hurting himself.

- Electrical wires should be enclosed completely. There should not be any loose wires near the cage, especially on the floor. If someone accidentally trips on it and tips the cage over, it can be bad news for your bird.

- All the toilet lids and any water container in your home should be covered. There have been several reports of Amazon Parrots and other species of parrots drowning accidentally.

- The cage should be away from the kitchen. There are fumes, especially those released by Teflon pans, which can be toxic for your bird. Prolonged exposure to these fumes can cause serious health issues.

- It is best to have a kitchen with a door that can be closed every time the bird is out of the cage. Hot stove tops and utensils are the number one cause of injuries in birds.

- Do not have doors that can close automatically. There are chances that your bird will get caught in between when the door is shutting.

- Table fans should be kept out of the bird's way. Make sure that all fans, table or ceiling, are powered off when your bird is let out of the cage.

- Always check doors and windows when you leave your home. You do not want your bird to get away if you leave the house with one of them open.

- Make sure you check if a certain plant is toxic to your bird or not when you place it near the cage of the bird.

- The cage doors should have a secure lock. A simple latch does not hold an Amazon Parrot back as they will soon figure out how to let themselves out. Do not forget that you are dealing with a very intelligent bird. They are also powerful enough to just rip the lock apart.

The safer the environment, the less stressed your bird will be. You will also not have to worry about untoward incidents that will leave your bird with serious injuries. Even after all the precautions have been taken, make sure that you never leave the bird out of his cage without proper supervision.

Chapter 5: Top 12 Questions of New Parrot Owners

If you are new to the world of parrots, you may have several questions about raising the bird. Here are the top 12 questions every new Amazon Parrot parent has:

1. How should the bird be transported?

In most cases, the bird is driven from the breeder's, the pet store or the shelter. Avoid having the bird shipped as they can develop health issues as they are put under a lot of stress. If you are driving your bird home, here are some tips that you should follow:

- Get the bird accustomed to the ambience of your car. Transfer him to a travel cage and place the cage in the car for a few minutes. You can leave the windows down or can turn the air conditioner on at room temperature.

- Never leave the bird in a hot car. In many states, this is considered illegal and is viewed as cruelty against the bird.

- Get the bird used to the movement. Drive around the block and watch the bird's body language.

- If he is singing and perched in an erect posture, he is quite unfazed by the movement of the car. He could even get on to the floor if the perch is shaky. But, the body language will be positive.

- If your bird is trembling and has retreated to one corner of the cage, stop the car. Put him in his cage with lots of food and water. Try again after sometime.

- As the bird gets more comfortable, you can increase the distance of your drive.

- Ensure that there is a lot of clean drinking water available for your bird. You must also have fresh pellets in a bowl for him to eat on the way. The substrate should be thick and have multiple layers. Your bird is likely to poop more when he is travelling.

- Make sure that you stop the car every half an hour to give the bird a break. He will be able to stop, drink some water and refresh himself. On the way, keep the air-conditioner on at room temperature and keep the cage away from any drafts.

- Do not keep the window open as it freaks the bird out. Lastly, place the cage in the shade. Or you could put a towel over half the cage as a retreat spot for your bird. The cage should be kept in a way that prevents too much movement.

- Avoid loud music. You must also avoid talking to the bird during your drive home.

The second option is transporting the bird by air. In this case, here are a few things to keep in mind.

- Before you look for airlines that will let you travel with your bird, you need to make sure that your Amazon Parrot is allowed to enter a certain state or country. There are strict laws with respect to importing exotic parrot species in several parts of the world.

- Contacting the Wildlife and Fisheries Authority in the country or state that you are travelling to will help you understand the legal considerations. You can also visit the official website of CITES to understand the laws that apply to your bird when crossing borders.

- If there is any paperwork that needs to be done, make sure that you plan at least 6 months in advance. You do not want any delays to cause problems in your travel plans.

- If the bird is allowed to enter a state or country, he will require a health certificate. This should be made not more than 30 days before your travel dates.

- Contact an airline that allows pets on board. You will have to purchase a carrier that is approved by the airlines.

- When you are ready to travel, line the carrier with enough bedding and leave a toy for your bird to have something familiar with him. Water should be provided in bottles to prevent dampness and related infections.

- The airlines will be able to feed your bird at regular intervals. Of course, there is an additional service charge for this. Make sure that the cage is secured properly and the door is shut tight.

- Having the bird checked within 24 hours of reaching the new home will be beneficial. There could be minor stress related health issues that can be treated easily. Even if your bird seems perfectly healthy, a good check-up is mandatory.

In most cases, the breeder or pet store will help you with all the formalities with respect to air travel. The only thing you need to make sure is that the bird is in good condition when he begins to travel. This means, you need a health certificate and a thorough report of the medical exam sent to you before the bird is transported.

2. How to keep the bird comfortable on the first day?

The first day of your bird in your home is very critical. In fact, the first week is very important to help the bird create positive associations with his new space. If not, there are chances that he will take longer to build trust and bond with you and your family.

The first thing you need to do is make sure that the bird is allowed to calm down. You need to prepare his new enclosure. Place it in a room that is rather quiet. This room should be away from any main road where there could be a lot of noise due to traffic. The bird must feel secure. So, place this cage against a wall. Do not keep it in an area like the hallway as there is too much commotion. You definitely do not want to place it in the family room or the living room. The bird should be in a space that allows him to observe his new home and family without really getting in the middle of all the action.

Make plenty of food available for the bird. Keep fresh water in the cage too. The first day should not include any interaction. As a new pet owner, you may be excited to fondle and cuddle the bird. But, it will only damage the health of your bird. Just walk past his cage, follow your normal routine but do not talk to him or interact with him.

You must make sure that you keep children away from the cage for the first few days. It is a good idea to cover one part of the cage with a towel. This can become the bird's hiding place or sleeping area. It will also protect him from the light of the television and any other light in your home.

The next morning, you can simply change the food and water in the cage. Do not talk to the bird still. Just casually go about the cleaning and feeding and let your bird observe you. A bird that is already socialized will probably not be afraid of you. However, if your bird is reclusive and in one corner of the cage, he is probably still scared.

The most important thing to do would be to prepare your family and tell them that they will have to let the bird get acclimatized before they interact with the new member of the family. It is also a good idea to bring the bird home when you are in all day. Do not bring him if you know that he is going to be all alone on a particular day. That will only scare him a lot more in this brand new environment. While there should not be any interaction, the bird should be able to watch and observe your family.

3. When can interactions with the bird begin?
For about 1 week, keep the interactions with your Amazon Parrot minimal. Then, you can start by saying a few words to the bird as you pass by the cage or even just sitting near the cage for a few minutes each day.

Make sure you pass by the cage often. That way, your bird will get accustomed to your presence. You will also be interacting with the bird when you are feeding him and cleaning the cage. This is the bonding time.

After a day or two, you can say words like "Hello" and "Bye" in a very soft and soothing voice. With an Amazon Parrot, do not be surprised if he responds with the same words.

Once you think that the bird is ready, you can start actual interactions. You will know that your bird is ready by observing his body language. His posture will be erect. He will use the perch. His level of activity will increase. Also, when you approach the cage to feed him, he will not cover himself or retreat behind the towel. That indicates that your bird is getting used to your home. With Amazon Parrot birds, this will happen much faster than any other parrot species because they are naturally very social creatures.

Now, you can sit by the cage and talk to your bird in a calm voice. Just place your hands on the wall of the cage for a while and sit in front of the cage quietly. The bird will approach your hand, lick it and probably even nibble at it. This is a good sign as it shows that your bird is not afraid of you. You can even move your hand around the walls and see if the bird follows your hand. If he does, then he is warming up to you.

When you are interacting with your bird, make sure that you are at his eye level at all times. When you are feeding, cleaning or even just talking to him, stay at the same level as him. If you tower over the cage, he will view you as a predator and will get scared of you. He will also assume that you mean harm if he feels like you are much larger than him in size.

Staying at eye level, on the other hand, tells him that you are part of his flock and that you are both equals in the group. This will help him trust you more and approach you more positively.

4. Are there any basic rules to lay down?

Make sure that all family members are informed about the difficulties that birds face during the transition period. Here are some ground rules that you can lay down for all members of the family:

- They will not tease or play with the bird.
- No loud music or television should be allowed in the house till the bird is at ease.
- No visitors in your home.
- If there are any large and colorful objects in the room that you have placed the cage in, take it out immediately.
- If your home has multiple birds or other pets, you will not introduce them to the new bird.
- The new bird needs to be left alone.

You can ease off on these rules once the bird is comfortable in your home. Then the other members of the family can be allowed to interact freely with the birds, too.

5. Is it safe to have an Amazon Parrot Around my child?

If you have a newborn baby in your home, it is advised that you do not bring home an Amazon Parrot. They both require a lot of attention. If you are unable to give the bird the attention he needs, he may grow jealous of the baby and may even attack the child.

Now, if you already have an Amazon Parrot and then have a baby, never go to the bird after the baby is put away in the crib. Then the Amazon Parrot gets a message that he is loved only when the baby is away. That leads to jealousy and anger. Such a bird will attack the baby or may start exhibiting behavior such as feather plucking. Make sure that you go about your daily routine with the bird while the baby is in the room. It is not a good idea to let the bird out of the cage, though.

If you want to bring an Amazon Parrot home to teach your child responsibility, you must wait until the child is older. This is a good pet for pre-teens or teenagers. If you have a little one at home who is younger than 7 years of age, it is not advisable to leave him alone with the bird. These birds have powerful beaks. That is something you must never underestimate. These beaks are strong and sharp and can inflict serious damage upon anyone. Most often birds like Amazon Parrots that are so social will be kind and gentle towards everyone in the family. But if you cross a line, he will let you know. Now, with a child who is less than 7 years of age this could happen by accident, leading to serious injuries.

It is a rule of the thumb that larger parrots are easier to form relationships with. So, if you have had a budgie or a cockatiel, it is not the same as having an Amazon Parrot. These birds need a lot more work to turn them into great companions. If you are patient enough, you will have a friend for life. Even if you are a first time owner or if you have a child in your home who wants an Amazon Parrot, you can both build very successful relationships with the bird if you are willing to learn and be patient with him. But a child must not be allowed to do this unsupervised.

Children tend to get scared easily and may react with a scream when the bird is being playful. In some cases, children could just get naughty and tease the bird. Both these situations are negative for your parrot and he will react by either nipping or attacking the child. The bird is not to be blamed as he is only responding by instinct. You cannot blame the child because, well, he is a child. As an adult, you need to be very responsible about introducing your bird to the child at the appropriate age.

6. Can household pets become friends with the parrot?

Cats and dogs are predators by the natural order. That already makes them a threat to your Amazon Parrot irrespective of how sweet and friendly they are towards people.

During the first few days, allow the bird to become aware of the presence of the other animal. Let him watch and observe your pet cat or dog. There must be no surprises later on. Just make sure that your dog or cat does not approach the cage while you are away. Your cat, especially, should not be allowed to climb over the cage.

When the bird seems settled in, it is time for the introductions. While keeping the bird in the cage, you will let the dog or cat around it. Let them sniff and explore. If your dog begins to bark or if your cat becomes aggressive, separate them instantly.

Now, keep doing this until your dog or cat is used to the bird. That will make them ignore the new member of the family even when in the same room. When you have reached this stage, it may be safe to let the bird out and interact with the pets

You can take this liberty only when your dog or cat has been trained well to heel. When these animals are trained, the risk to the bird is reduced to a large extent as you will be able to control your cat or dog even if they just get too excited.

If you see that your pet cat or dog is chasing the bird around, you must put the bird back in the cage. In case your bird is not hand trained, wrap a towel around his body and your hands while handling him.

In any case, it is never advisable to leave the bird alone with your pets. While they may seem to get along with each other perfectly well in your presence, do not take any risks.

A dog can seriously harm the Amazon Parrot with a simple friendly nibble. At the same time, an Amazon Parrot is powerful enough to rip the dog's ear right off when provoked. As for cats, the biggest threat is the saliva of the cat which is poisonous for any bird.

Remember that you are dealing with highly instinctive creatures. You can never be sure of when their instinctive behavior will kick in. So, it is best that you let them interact in your presence. In case there are any signs of aggression, it is best to keep your Amazon Parrot confined in the presence of the cat or the dog.

7. If I have other birds, how to safely introduce a new bird?

The first and most important thing is to quarantine your new bird. He should be kept in a separate room entirely for at least 30 days. This will allow you to check for any health issues. Even if the bird is a carrier, you will be able to prevent any disease spreading throughout the flock with proper quarantining measures.

When you have quarantined the bird, make sure that you do not interact with the other birds after you have interacted with him. This means that the existing flock should be fed and cleaned first. If you must interact with the existing flock after you have spent time with the quarantined bird, make sure that you wash your hands thoroughly.

Introduce the birds one after the other after the quarantine period is over. Start with the bird who is the calmest of the lot. Place him and the new bird in separate carriers, next to each other. You can let them out and observe the behavior when you are around to supervise.

If there is an aggressive response, try again. If not put the birds back in and then keep them with each other for a few days. Repeat this with all the birds in the cage so they are familiar with each other.

Once this is done, put the birds in the cage together and let them be. Unless you see any aggressive behavior, you can let the birds be. Small squabbles are natural as the flock is simply establishing a pecking order among them.

Remember that with any bird, making introductions during the bluffing phase is not a good idea. It will lead to some nasty fights. Younger birds are easiest to introduce to the flock as they will not be perceived as a threat.

8. What does an Amazon Parrot Eat?

Your bird needs a well-balanced diet that comprises of:

Seeds

Seeds have always been the center of debate when it comes to the Amazon Parrot's diet. It is true that your bird's diet should never entirely comprise of seeds. However, there are seasonal seeds that are good for your bird. The commercially available bird seeds are very high in fat and low in essential nutrients. They might lead to obesity or metabolic issues in your bird.

Seed consumption must be limited. They are highly palatable and are extremely good tools for training the bird. But they should form the smallest part of your bird's diet. If your bird has been on a seed only diet at the breeder's you can get him to eat pellets by mixing the two. Then, increase the pellet portion and reduce the seeds gradually. Your bird will eventually learn to love a seed based diet.

Pellets

These are the most essential part of your bird's diet. Pellets have several specially created formulations that ensure best nutrition for your bird. You will get special pellets to help birds through different stages of growth such as molting, sexual maturity, brooding etc. Some of them are also specially formulated to act as catalysts for certain medical treatments.

Pellets must form 75-80% of your bird's diet. So weaning the bird off is necessary. If you see sudden changes in the health of your bird when you wean him from seeds, consult your vet. He will also be able to help you with the right brand to give your bird.

Fruits and vegetables

Fresh produce should make up 20% of your bird's diet. If you give your birds vegetables that are only rich in water, the nutritional value is very low. Choose bright and pulpy fruits for the best result.

Make sure that you wash the produce well before feeding it to the bird. You can cut them into small pieces depending upon the bite size of your bird. It is recommended that you heat them up a little bit to make them more appealing to the bird. The skin can be left on usually. Amazon Parrots are very clever birds. They will pick their favorites and will refuse to eat other fruits and vegetables. Make sure you give them a large variety of fruits and veggies to help them choose. Of course, avocado should be left out of this list as it is toxic to your bird.

It is a good idea to start the day with a bowl of pellets. Then, you can feed the fruits and vegetables to the bird after a gap of 2 to 3 hours. This will ensure that your bird will eat all the varieties of foods that you are giving him and not just his personal favorites.

Now, the thing with parrots is that they should watch their flock eat a certain food before they eat it. So, if you want to introduce the bird to a new fruit, eat it in front of him and be very expressive about how delicious the fruit is. This will make him want to eat it too.

You must change the diet as per the stage of life your bird is in. Make sure that you consult your vet about the requirements of your bird before you make these changes. If you are giving your bird fortified pellets, supplementation is not really necessary. If your bird is tested as deficient in certain nutrients like calcium, you can give him supplements. You will get supplements that are soluble in water and also available as chew toys.

Make sure that clean water is always available for your birds. Drinking water is the only way that the nutrients that he consumes are transported throughout the body. You may offer foods from your plate as long as you know that it is good for your bird.

It is recommended that you change the pellets every day. Even if it means that you need to throw away most of the pellets from the previous day, you need to do it. Of course, fruits and veggies that are close to rotting should never be given to the bird or even left in the cage. Monitor your bird's eating habits every day. If you notice an unusual increase or decrease in the food consumed, you will have to consult your vet immediately. Also keep the food and water bowls clean. Amazon Parrots are very picky and will not eat or drink from a dirty dish.

9. How often should the cage be cleaned?

Cage maintenance consists of two parts; daily cleaning and weekly or fortnightly cleaning.

Daily cleaning

The food and water containers must be cleaned on a daily basis. If you use steel or porcelain ones, they are easiest to clean. It is a good idea to keep a spare pair that you can use when the ones that you have washed are drying. Use a cleansing gel that you can get in a pet store to clean the bowl. Then, rinse it with water thoroughly. Never leave any chemicals behind as it may seriously harm your bird. These bowls need to be fully dry before they are replaced.

The substrate needs to be removed and replaced on a daily basis. Most of the moisture is retained in the substrate and should be removed to prevent any fungal or bacterial growth.

Any surface that is exposed must be wiped down on a daily basis. You can use disinfectants in a very dilute form, spray it on the surface and then wipe it down after leaving it on for about 10 minutes. This is one way to make sure that your cage is sanitized and clean. In addition to that, it also increases the life of the cage.

Weekly or fortnightly cleaning

It is a good idea to remove all the toys from the cage every fortnight and clean them thoroughly. Any severely damaged ones can be thrown away. Use a brush to remove any dry organic matter. If you notice that one of the toys is very dirty wash it immediately and dry it before replacing it. Soak the toys in a cleansing solution and rinse them completely. No chemical from the cleaning agent should be left behind as it is harmful for your bird. Then, make sure that they are fully dry before you put them back in the cage.

Make it a monthly practice to wash the cage out thoroughly. You will have to use a brush to scrub out any dry material from the floor or the cage.

Using warm water makes it easier to clean the dirty parts of the cage very easily. You can simply use a soap water solution. Then, wash and rinse the cage fully. Once it is dry, spray a disinfectant and wash it down. Of course, you will have to have a stand by enclosure for your bird. Do not put the bird back until the cage is fully dry.

Some of you may want to keep the cage outdoors. Then you must wash the whole cage twice a month. That will make sure that any pathogens that have been released into the cage by wild birds or rodents will be removed. It will also keep dust at bay.

If your bird has not been hand trained, you will need to use a towel to handle the bird. Wrap the towel around his body. Allow the ends to fall over your hands and protect them from any bites. Make sure that the head is not covered by the cloth. You can also use sturdy gloves to protect yourself from accidents.

The cage that you transfer your bird to must have a lot of food and water if this is the first time. Once the bird is trained and accustomed to this routine, it will be a lot easier for you. In case you are unsure of what cleansing agent you can use, consult your vet first. It is recommended that you check the cage thoroughly every day. In case you find any debris or peculiar droppings, clean it instantly. You definitely do not want to leave pieces of rotting food around. With all species of parrots, you will also have to clean out the things that they hoard in their cage as part of their nesting habits.

10. Is my bird really happy?

The body language of your bird can tell you a lot about his mental state. Here are some signs to look for to understand how your bird is actually feeling. That way, you will know if your bird is really happy or not.

Eyes
- The eyes of the bird will dilate depending upon the level of excitement, curiosity, anger or fear.
- This is called pinning or flashing.
- Make sure that you take in the context of the environment around your bird and his general body posture to understand exactly what the bird is trying to communicate with his eyes.

Wings

- The bird will flap his wings as a form of exercise in most cases.
- Flapping the wings is also a way to get your attention simply because your bird is happy to see you.
- Flipping the wing is a sign of pain or anger. If you cannot see any stimulus for either, then the bird is probably just fluffing up his feathers.
- Drooping wings are a sign of fatigue. If the wings droop even when the bird is resting, it is a sign that your bird is unwell.

Tail

- Like any other animal, the tail is an important medium of communication.
- Wagging the tail indicates that your bird is happy.
- If he fans out his tail feathers, the bird is trying to show dominance by looking larger. This is done during the breeding season or just before he is going to attack.
- Bobbing of the tail after play and exercise indicates that the bird is just trying to catch his breath.
- Bobbing of the tail otherwise is an indication of respiratory issues

Leg and feet

- Tapping the feet is often seen as a sign of aggression in your bird. He does this to assert dominance.
- The legs will appear weak after you have played with your bird and are putting him back in the cage. This is no cause for worry as the bird is just resisting going back in to the cage.

Beak

- Grinding of the beak shows that your bird is happy and content.
- If he clicks the beak once, he is simply greeting you and saying hello.
- Multiple clicks on the other hand are a sign of warning and it is best that you stay away from your bird.

Body posture

- If the body of the bird is erect and alert but the muscles are relaxed, it shows that he is happy.
- An alert body with stiff muscles means that the bird is showing dominance and is probably going to attack.

Vocalization

- Sounds like chattering, whistling and singing are a sing of contentment in your bird.
- Growling and purring indicates aggression or disapproval.
- Clicking of the tongue means that he wants to play with you.

These signs will become clearer as you interact with your bird. You will also see certain movements and body postures unique to your bird which will help you understand what he wants.

11. What if the bird escapes?

Sometimes the cage may be left open or not secured properly. In these cases, the bird may escape. If you are lucky, the bird will stay indoors. However, in case there is an open window or door, it might become an issue. If you are present when the bird is just about to fly away, you can do the following:

- Call out your bird's name loudly as he begins to fly. Birds are great at tracking sounds and are likely to get back to you when they hear you.

- Do not look away from your bird and keep your eyes on him for as long as you can. You will be able to tell how far he was able to get, the direction he went in and the possible area that he landed in if you do this.

- Call your friends and family immediately and try to get them to the spot. The more people you have searching for the bird, the easier he will be to find.

If your bird has already escaped, then you will find these tips helpful:
- Look around in the area that you saw the bird last in. You can cover a bigger radius if you have more people looking for the bird.

- There could be several phrases or sounds that your bird is familiar with. Shout them out along with the name of the bird as you are calling out to him. A lost bird will most likely call back when he hears you. He is definitely afraid and is trying to relocate his flock.

- If you have any recording of your parrot screaming on your phone, play it out, He may respond to this too.

- If your parrot has a mate or a cage mate that he is closely bonded to, take the bird along in a cage and place him in the area that you last saw your parrot in. Stay away from this cage and wait. If the bird in the cage screams or shouts because you are away, the lost bird may respond.

- If you do not find the bird in this area, increase your search radius by 1 mile. It is very unlikely that your parrot would have gone too far away. Only when the wind is too strong or if the bird has been chased by a predator will he get too far from home.

- In many cases, your bird may see you and become absolutely quiet. This is because he feels scared in your presence. So don't just rely on sound or a call back and keep searching for the bird with your eyes.

- Look for movement rather than color. Even with the bright plumes of the Amazon Parrot, you just may not be able to see him on a tree or behind bushes.

If the bird has been gone for a whole day or more, you may have to seek professional assistance to get your bird back. There are a few organizations that you can call for help including:

- The local animal control
- SPCA or the humane society
- Your Vet
- Local zoos
- Pet shops around your area
- The local police.
- You may place an advertisement in the classifieds section of papers.
- You must also constantly check the found section of classifieds to see if anyone has found your bird.
- Post several flyers of the lost bird around the neighborhood.

Make sure you continue to look for your bird. There have been instances when the bird has flown back voluntarily to find his flock.

12. What if I have to travel?

If you cannot take your bird along with you on your trip, you have the option of getting a friend or relative to watch the bird. You will have to make some arrangements for your bird while you are away to ensure that he is being cared for properly

The first option is to ask a friend or a relative to pitch in to take care of your bird. If they can stay in your home and do so, it is the best option for the bird. It is less stressful for your birds. Make sure that the person you ask is completely trustworthy.

In case you are unable to find someone who can make time for the bird, the next option is to ask your vet if he has a pet hostel facility where your bird can stay while you are away. He may be able to recommend a reliable option if he doesn't. Make sure that you go and check the facility out if this is the first time the bird is going there.

The last measure that you can take is hire a pet sitter. There are several professional agencies such as the Pet Sitters International and the National Association of Pet Sitters where you can look for a pet sitter in your area.

The National association of Professional Pet Sitters lays down some guidelines that will help you find a good sitter for your bird:

- The sitter must have a commercial liability insurance. Then, in case there is some problem with your bird you may hold them responsible for it.

- Ask for recommendations from previous clients. A good sitter will not have any problem connecting you with them.

- Make sure that all the costs involved are on paper. That way neither of you is in the dark about the possible expenditure.

- Meet the person who will be sitting your bird and introduce your bird to them.

- While you are interviewing them, keep an eye on their behavior with the bird. If they are comfortable and easy going with the bird, then it is likely that they have good experience too.

- All the services that the sitter will provide should be mentioned in the agreement. One important clause is with respect to the vet. In case your bird falls sick or has an emergency, the sitter that you hire must be able to deal with it efficiently.

- What will the sitter do if he is unable to show up due to illness or any other emergency? Make sure that he or she has a backup.

Once you are satisfied with all the answers provided by the sitter, you need to make a contract. Ensure that you leave a list of things that he or she may feed the bird, details of any illnesses and lastly, the number of your avian vet with the sitter.

The first time you leave your bird is the hardest. You will eventually get accustomed to one pet sitter who can take care of all your bird's needs. It is best to find a sitter who will stay at your place and take care of the bird. This reduces a lot of stress on the part of your Amazon Parrot.

Travelling is one of the biggest points for consideration when you bring home an Amazon Parrot. If you are a frequent traveler, do not bring a bird home.

When you have to take decisions like moving out of a country, think about your Amazon Parrot. If your bird cannot go with you, are you willing to put him in foster care? If not, then you will have to make compromises on your travel for this. Only when you are willing to make these sacrifices should you bring an Amazon Parrot home.

Chapter 6: Bonding with Amazon Parrots

One of the most important things for any Amazon Parrot owner is to ensure that they form a strong bond with their bird. The more you interact and play with the bird, the more you will stay connected with one another. Of course, basic training is a must if you want to be able to include your bird in more activities with you.

Training and bonding with Amazon Parrots can be extremely fulfilling, not just for the bird but for you as well.

1. Training your Amazon Parrots

Since Amazon Parrots have excellent cognitive ability, they respond very well to training. Basic training is extremely important. Once you get the hang of it, you will be able to get your bird to perform several tricks as well. You can be as creative as you want with advanced training as it is a great way to keep your bird mentally stimulated.

Start by building trust

For the bird to respond to training, he should be able to trust you first. This is a slow process but once you have managed it, it can be extremely rewarding. Start by just spending a few minutes every day, talking to the bird and just placing your hand on the walls of the enclosure.

If you are the one feeding him every day, he is likely to bond faster. If your bird begins to respond by approaching your hand, licking it or nibbling at it slowly, it is a good sign. You can then start offering treats through the bars of the cage. If your bird does not eat it, just leave it in the cage and keep trying. Once the bird accepts a treat from your hand, the next step is to let him out of the cage.

Just open the cage door and let the bird come out. He will probably climb up on the cage and just explore the space around. Make sure that the space is safe for your bird and free from threats like pets or ceiling fans.

Then, you can hold out some treats in your hand and see if the bird will approach your hand. When your bird starts eating comfortably from your hand, it means that he is tamed enough to start the actual training.

Putting the bird back is easy. Just leave a few of his favorite treats or toys in the cage and he will go to them. In case your bird is reluctant to go into the cage before he is hand tamed, use toweling to handle him. Wrap his body with a thick towel and let the ends fall over your hand. Then, pick him up gently holding the wings down and put him back in the cage. Treats and toys will help him understand that the cage is a fun place to be in.

Get the bird to step up

Teaching your Amazon Parrot to step up on your finger or on a perch makes him more hand tamed. Besides that, a bird who will willingly step up is easier to rescue from an unsavory situation such as a fight with a household pet or even an accident such as a fire in the house. Here are a few simple steps to begin step up training with your bird.

- If your bird is hand tamed, you can expect him to step up right away. If not, you have to first make him comfortable enough to approach your hand.

- Holding a treat through the cage bars is the first step. Then you can work your way towards opening the door and using the treat to lure the bird out of the cage.

- When the bird is comfortable with approaching you, you can hold out your finger like a perch or use an actual one.

- Then, hold a treat just behind the perch or your finger and wait for the bird to step up voluntarily before handing it out to him. Use the cue "Up" or "Step up" every time you do so.

- Do not be surprised if the bird tries to get his beak around your finger. He is only making sure that the perch is steady. Withdrawing the hand sharply will make him lose trust.

- Once the bird has stepped up, offer the treat and then set him back in the cage with another treat or toy.

- You can slowly try to hold him on the finger or perch and get him out of the cage and walk around for a while. Remember, when you put him back, make it a positive experience by providing treats.

- You can do the same to get him to step up on your shoulder or head once he is comfortable.

- Eventually, the bird will respond to the cue and will not require a treat in order to step up.

Teaching your parrot to talk

Amazon Parrots are among the best talkers in the world of parrots. They are able to pick up a lot of the human vocabulary by simply listening to their humans.

If you say words like "Hello" and "Goodbye" often to your bird, you will be surprised at how quickly the bird picks up these simple words. Of course with a bird that has the talking ability of an Amazon Parrot, you do not want to limit the vocabulary. Training your parrot to talk is quite simple and extremely rewarding.

Here are a few tips to teach your parrot new words:

- Pick a word that you want to teach him. Suppose you pick, "Hello", you need to say this everyday at a specific time.

- Make sure there are no distractions like TV sounds when you are saying the word that you want to teach him.

- Now associate that with an action that he will remember, like you walking into a room.

- Say it in a high pitched sound and sound as excited as you can.

- If you are super excited, he will feel motivated to learn that call as it is positive to him.

- Eventually, when you enter the room, he will respond with a high pitched, "Hello". Be patient.

Birds merely mimic what we say. So repeating words and phrases before the bird is the best way to train them to talk. When your parrot picks a word up, give him loads of treats and praise him abundantly.

Speaking to the bird every day and saying the words that you want him to learn in a high and excited voice will make him pick up on it. Another great idea to get your bird to learn words is to play the radio and also cartoons to him. He will pick up on words that he hears often.

You will also notice your bird mumbling these words to himself before he actually says them out loud. This is his way of practicing what he has learnt. It seems like your bird is actually chattering to himself when he is learning words.

Potty training Amazon Parrots

If you plan to let your bird out of the cage, potty training can save you from hours of cleaning up after your bird. This is a harder behavior to teach your bird. However, with consistency, you will notice that the bird will only poop in places where he is "allowed" to.

Here are some simple tricks to teach your bird to poop where you want them to.

- The first thing to do would be to teach him to poop inside the cage in the morning.

- Before feeding, put paper on the floor of the cage and wait for the bird to poop.

- They will show a very distinct type of body language which is usually lifting their tail and leaning down on the perch. Then, when they do poop, praise them abundantly and offer a treat which is part of the diet.

- The next step is to watch for these signs after you have taught your bird to step up.

- When you see the pooping body language, hold them over a trash can or over a piece of paper. Then when they do poop on that, they need to be praised abundantly.

- That way, they know that there is one place or appropriate place for them to poop and they will not mess the whole house up.

Amazon Parrots can learn great tricks picking up cards, and even solving simple puzzles. You can look for suggestions online. If you are part of any local Amazon Parrot club, you can find great ideas from other owners, too!

2. Grooming Amazon Parrots

Grooming is a great way to keep your bird clean and healthy. Grooming is also necessary to keep your bird safe. For example, wing clipping will prevent your bird from flying away or having accidents. But, above all, grooming requires you to spend time with your bird. This builds a great deal of trust between you and your Amazon Parrot as well. As a result, grooming is extremely important as a bonding activity.

Bathing

Parrots require regular bathing in order to stay healthy. They may even take a dip in their water bowl once in a while to keep themselves cool. But, you need to make it a point to give your bird a bath every 15 days in order to keep his feathers clean and free from any matting.

You need not use any soap on your bird unless there is any debris or dirt on the feathers. It is a good idea to consult your vet before using a certain soap on your bird. Some of them may have chemicals that are toxic for your bird. Use soap locally on the area that is dirty and rinse it gently with warm water.

The best way to bathe your bird is to mist his feathers. If he enjoys it, he will lift his feathers and move around allowing you to continue. On the other hand, if he begins to crouch or back away, it means that he does not like it. Never spray directly on the bird's face.

You can also use a shallow water bath to let your bird take a dip. Let the bird step up on your finger. Then lower your hand till the bird just touches the water a little. If your bird wants to take a bath, he will hop in. If you want to urge him to take a bath, you can also put some spinach leaves in the water. The bird will hop in and chew on the leaves while taking a bath.

Misting your Amazon Parrot is a great idea. Since these birds are from the rainforests, a light drizzle of water or even holding the bird under a warm shower is enjoyable for the bird.

Wing Clipping

Wing Clipping is necessary if you do not want to have any flight related accidents at home. This may also lead to escape and loss of your parrot.

If you have pets at home, do not clip the wings. This is your bird's only form of defense. Even when you have multiple birds in an aviary, the wings should be intact to help your bird escape an aggressive cage mate.

If you decide to clip your bird's wings, make sure you have it done at the vet's the first time. You can learn how to do it, practice with your vet and then do it at home. You need to be very experienced to ensure that you do not accidentally clip any blood feathers.

A bird must be hand tamed before you decide to clip his wings yourself. He must be comfortable enough to let you handle him. The first thing is to get your bird into a comfortable position to clip his wings. Pick him up using a towel and place him face down on your thigh. Then let the first wing out of the loose end of the towel and spread the feathers. Cut the primary feathers only. These are the largest feathers. The first three feathers are usually cut. You can snip about 1cm from each feather.

Then, repeat on the other side. Compare the wings to make sure that they are equal. If they are not, your bird will have difficulty walking or even perching. In case you do get a blood feather, make sure you apply styptic power to the wound immediately. If the bleeding does not stop, take the pet to the vet to have the shaft removed.

Clipping the wings only reduces your bird's ability to fly. It does not prevent flight altogether. So, when you take your bird outdoors, be vigilant. Even the slightest breeze can give him the lift he needs and lead to an escape. You need to clip the wings every 6 months. With these playful birds, trimming of toe nails or beaks is not needed as they will do it themselves by scraping the sharp surfaces off on any rough object like the wooden perch.

Beak and toenail trimming
This grooming process is optional. If you notice that your bird's toes and beak are getting stuck in the toys or any fabric, you can trim them to avoid any accidents. If the beak or toe of your bird is stuck to the fabric on your sofa and he tries to move suddenly, there are chances that the whole toe rips off or the beak is severely damaged. To avoid this, trim the sharp ends.

Wrap the bird with a towel, only exposing the part that you want to trim. In the case of the beak, gently lift the upper mandible with your finger and feel the sharp end. Keep the beak supported and trim the beak using a nail file. When you feel that it is just blunt, stop trimming. If the nail or the toe is too short, the bird will be unable to climb and hold properly.

Even with the toe, make sure that you have a finger supporting the nail you want to trim to avoid any chances of breakage or unwanted damage.

Usually with Amazon Parrots, beak trimming is necessary, as the end gets very sharp and pointy. However, do not trim the beak too much as the bird actually uses the beak as a third limb. This means that activities such as climbing and even feeding require the beak to be in good shape. If it is too blunt, these activities are deterred.

3. Play with your bird
Playing with your bird is a lot of fun. Amazon Parrots are quite goofy by nature. You can figure out games that your bird loves and can also give them a lot of toys that will help keep them active and stimulated.

Foraging is one of the Amazon Parrot's most favorite forms of play. They will simply love the foraging toys that you can buy in stores. If you plan to give them these toys, be prepared to replace them often. Amazon Parrots are very smart and will figure the toy out in no time. Once that happens, foraging is no longer fun. That is when your creativity comes to play. Make sure that you include foraging activities in their routine. This could mean looking for a treat in a gap in one of the old toys, a corner of the cage etc. They will really enjoy the experience of hunting down their favorite treat.

One form of play that we often neglect is "observation". Parrots love to watch people and imitate them. They will listen to your conversations very intently. So, once your parrot is accustomed to your home, you need to spend time talking to him. Honestly, it feels like you are talking to another human being.

Toys that make noises are also appreciated by Amazon Parrots. They get really excited when you give them toys that make a sound upon pushing a button or when you move the toy. You can actually pass a few of your child's toys to the parrot and watch him get just as excited as your baby. If you plan to use children's toys, make sure that the casing is very sturdy and that the batteries do not fall out easily. The battery is toxic for your little bird. It should also not have small parts that the parrot may swallow.

Basically, parrots love the idea of manipulating objects with their beaks. This includes untying knots, twisting knobs or just playing with beads. As long as it is fiddly and time consuming, your bird will love it.

Toys you can try
The market is flooded with several toys that you can buy for your bird. These toys are either available online or can be bought from your local pet store. Here are some fun options for your bird:

- **Foraging barrels:** You can place treats inside these barrels and let your bird just look for them and pick them out. These barrels are rather deep and are fun for your bird. You will get these barrels in various sizes to suit your parrot.

- **Claw reels:** You will get ready made cotton or plastic reels that can be suspended with a steel wire. These toys are handled by the birds using their claws. They simply love these soft and cushy reels that can be pulled and twisted.

- **Bells:** You can get special nickel plated hanging bells that are sturdy. These bells are usually made from the same material used to make bullet proof glass. These toys are noisy, can be pulled around and are very entertaining for your bird.
- **Leather towers:** Special chewing towers are made for your bird using leather. You can even make this at home by piling up layers of leather that is vegetable tanned. These towers are shredded and practically destroyed by the bird. You can even make a similar tower using palm leaves that your bird will love to shred into pieces. If this is not interesting, paper also works as a brilliant substitute.

You can get several other toys such as pacifiers that are made from beads and strings. Your Amazon Parrot is sure to love these toys. Just make sure that it is safe, free from any lead or lead based paint and durable. Make sure that the toys do not have a zinc plate either. This is very dangerous for your bird. Twine should never be used to hang the toys as it can cause cuts when the bird is flying around in the cage. No sharp edges in the cage; this is a rule that every parrot owner must follow to keep his beloved pet safe and secure.

Toys to avoid
Don't think that you will never go wrong with toys and play. There are some things that your Amazon Parrot will absolutely hate. Swings, for example, are not readily accepted by these birds. These toys are wobbly and the bird may have small mishaps with them. In any case, an Amazon Parrot does not appreciate new things thrown into the cage. They will approach anything new with a lot of caution, including toys.

So, when you place a swing, the parrot may avoid it initially. The good thing about Amazon Parrots is that they are really quick learners. They will be able to learn to balance themselves on the swing with regular practice. Do not force it upon them. Let them just enjoy the whole experience and take it one step at a time.

If you are bringing new toys for your bird, don't just place it in the cage. They do not appreciate new toys unlike cats and dogs. As mentioned before, these birds are contemplative. You must leave the toy outside the cage and let the bird just watch it for a while and explore it at its own pace when you let him out. If his reaction to this is positive, you can place it in the cage. If not, just avoid it.

Do not bring toys with big gaps and holes till your parrot is a little more skilled at using toys. This could lead to the head or the toes getting stuck in the gap, making the bird averse to toys altogether.

Handmade toy ideas

Toys can get expensive. With a bird like the Amazon Parrot, it is impossible to keep them pleased with the same old toy. They tend to get bored with toys that they have used several times. They do not even like toys that are "too easy". Remember, you are dealing with a highly intelligent creature. You need to get twice as creative if you want to keep them entertained.

You can make several toys at home to keep the bird interested. One of the easiest things to make is a foraging box. All you need to do is get a small box, seal it from all ends with just one end open. Then, stuff it with shredded paper and hide treats amidst the paper. Watch your bird forage around and have a great time. These boxes can even be suspended to make playtime more interesting for your bird.

If you do not have the time, you can simply wrap a paper tower with treats, add some layers and throw it into the cage. The bird will just rip the paper towel apart in pursuit of his favorite toy.

Bottle caps make very interesting toys for your bird. You can string a couple of them together and suspend them in the cage. The bird will tug and pull at these colorful caps. You can even hide a treat under one of the bottle caps and keep two empty ones. Shuffle the caps around and let your bird pick the one with the treat. This is great fun even for you.

If you are a wine lover, you are sure to have several corks lying around. Stitch a thread through the cork using a large needle. Make a few holes on the cork and stuff seeds into it. Hang this in the cage and your bird is sure to fall in love with it.

Besides this, you can use blocks of soft wood, paper and even leaves as chew toys for the bird. Hide treats around the cage or in one of the toys for your bird. Playing with an Amazon Parrot is all about creativity. The more you think, the more ideas you are likely to come up with. The only basics that you need to know is that the parrot loves to shred, chew, forage and pull. A toy that allows them to do one or more of the above will be adored.

Chapter 7: Breeding Amazon Parrots

Amazon Parrots should be bred only when they are at least 2 years old. Typically, owners and breeders wait till the bird is 3 years old. This is when they are sexually mature and ready to parent. These birds are monomorphic. This means that the male and the female look alike. So the first step is to learn how to distinguish a male from a female.

1. Telling the male and female apart

It is not possible to visually determine if you have a male or a female Amazon Parrot. There are two ways to determine the gender of the bird. Both require assistance from an avian vet. These methods include:

- **DNA sexing**
  This is the most common technique used to determine the gender of a bird. This method examines the DNA in your bird's sex chromosomes to tell them apart. It is also one of the most accurate methods used. In order to conduct this test, a "DNA probe" is required. A cloned form of the DNA fragment is obtained from the blood sample of the bird. The blood is usually drawn from the nail or from the feathers on the chest area.

  The sex chromosome of a male contains two Z chromosomes while females have one Z and one W chromosome. Since these chromosomes differ in their structure and size, they can be differentiated with a microscopic observation. The blood sample is submitted to a lab. The tests usually take between 7 to 9 days to be completed.

- **Surgical Sexing**
  This method is faster. It is also extremely reliable and safer than most other techniques. You need to make sure that your vet has ample experience with this method.

  The method involves a clear visualization of the reproductive organs of the bird. After the tests, the birds are provided with a tattoo to help prevent any confusion with respect to the gender of the bird.

  This method is not available with all vets as it requires mild anesthesia and a few simple surgical procedures. With large birds like the Amazon Parrot, the risk is reduced significantly. Unless your vet has performed these surgeries before, it is not advisable to have them done on your bird.

2. Introducing a mate to your bird

When you decide to introduce older birds to each other, the first thing to do is quarantine the new bird. Then, you must keep in mind that the female will be more aggressive and territorial than the male. These birds will dictate the whole relationship, the breeding season and also the rearing of the offspring.

So, if you have a female parrot, the introduction must happen in a new and neutral environment where the female is less likely to be territorial. Follow the same steps mentioned in the earlier chapters about the introduction of two birds.

The next thing to do is to check whether the birds are showing any bonding behavior. The first sign is that the birds are feeding each other. If you do not see this behavior, you can give them wood that they can chew.

This is a part of the courtship ritual and you will eventually see them starting to feed one another. Only when you see this consistently should you provide a nesting box.

Never provide a nesting box before the birds have bonded. This will make the female hide in the nesting box all day and your birds will most likely not mate. Even if the birds do mate, the eggs that are laid are clear. They will not produce any chicks when they hatch.

Once the nesting box has been introduced after the birds have bonded, the male will initiate mating. During this phase you need to give the birds a larger portion of food. This will allow them to believe that they can provide for their young when they are born. Avoid touching the birds during this time. Also, avoid loud music or any other stressful conditions for the birds.

In the first few days of introduction, you need to watch the birds extremely carefully. If you see that one of them is excessively aggressive towards the other, they may not be a compatible pair. Simply separate the birds. In case you are providing the bird with any supplement be very cautious. If one of them is getting an overdose of the supplement, he or she may become aggressive and hyperactive, leading you to believe that the birds are not compatible while they may actually be the perfect pair.

3. Preparing for the breeding season

Amazon Parrots generally breed in spring. They require very specific breeding conditions. On average, with every clutch, a female will lay 3-4 eggs.

Amazon Parrots are shy creatures and will not breed if there is too much disturbance. You need to first shift the cage of the birds to a room in the house that is quiet, but has a good supply of natural light. You can lay a cloth over the cage for the birds to escape into when they want to rest.

Unless there is a proper nesting place available for the birds, they are very unlikely to mate. Keeping a nesting box just outside the cage will encourage them to mate. The cage should be fixed at a height from the floor of the cage. It can be placed in the play area if you have a play top cage.

Instead of using cardboard boxes, it's best to get a store made nesting box for your Amazon Parrot. These nesting boxes made of wood or metal are not destroyed easily. They can be used for all the breeding seasons making the birds feel comfortable. These boxes are also easier to clean. You need to remember that Amazon Parrot chicks can be very messy.

Choose a vertical nesting box that measures at least 18X18X36 inches. These boxes usually have an entrance door and a separate inspection door that you can access.

The nesting box should be placed in such a way that the birds have a good view of the room around them. The cage should have solid perch for the birds. Place one inside the cage and one outside leading to the next box. This allows them to access the next. These perches should be made of hardwood as the females are likely to chew on them when they become hormonal.

Leaving a few soft wood options is a good idea to help the bird chew it and release some stress. With this arrangement, your birds will get ready to mate. The male will mount the female a couple of times. In two weeks the female will lay her first clutch of eggs that consists of 3-4 eggs that are white in color.

She will have a second clutch of eggs after a month. If you want the bird not to lay the second clutch you can reduce day time to about 10 hours. You can move the birds to a dark room or could just turn the light off early. Just when the bird is about to lay the first egg, her droppings become smelly and large. She will also show evident abdominal distension.

If you see that the hen is leaving the eggs dormant without sitting on them, you will have to increase the temperature of the nest using an aquarium heater. Parrots are known for abandoning their clutch. If you see that your bird does not sit on the eggs and incubate them even after increasing the temperature, you will have to incubate the eggs artificially.

If the hen does brood, the incubation period is about 26 days.

The incubation period is about 29 days, during which the hen will care for the eggs on her own.

Feeding the female

You need to make sure that the birds have adequate nutrients to produce the necessary hormones and have a successful breeding season. For the females, especially, the diet is of utmost importance.

Adding assorted nuts to the diet will help the bird to a large extent. Each nut has specific functions that aid the breeding season. Here are a few nuts that you should include and the benefits of these nuts:

-   Macadamia nuts- they provide the additional fats that are required in a bird's diet during this season.
-   Walnuts- they provide the birds with necessary omega 3 fatty acids.
-   Filberts- they are a great source of calcium for the females.
-   Pistachios- they aid vitamin A in large amounts.

In addition to that you can also provide coconut, eggs and fresh fruits and vegetables. The nutrition of the bird determines the final quality of the eggs that are produced during this season.

You can even provide fortified pellets or supplements under the guidance of your vet to give your birds the additional nutrition boost that they require.

4. Artificially hatching eggs

Most parrot species usually abandon their clutch after a few days. This is when you need to intervene and take care of the eggs yourself. Sometimes you will also notice that the hen also destroys a couple of the eggs.

To incubate the eggs, you can purchase a standard incubator from any pet supply store. You can also order them online. It is never advisable to prepare your own incubator as the temperature settings need to be very accurate to hatch the eggs successfully. The incubation period will be the same as the natural incubation period.

The incubator is a one-time investment that is completely worth it if you choose to breed more Amazon Parrots even in the next season.

Here are a few tips to incubate the eggs correctly:

- Pick the eggs up with clean hands. The chicks are extremely vulnerable to diseases and can be affected even with the smallest traces of microbes. Only pick eggs that are visibly clean. If there is a lot of debris or poop on a certain egg, it is best not to mix it with the other eggs as it will cause unwanted infections.

- Wash the eggs gently to clean the surface. The next step is to candle the eggs. This means you will have to hold the egg up to a light. If you can see the embryo in the form of a dark patch, it means that the egg is fertile. On the other hand, if all you can see is an empty space inside the egg, it is probably not going to hatch.

- In the natural setting, the eggs are usually given heat on one side while the other side remains cooler. Then the hen may turn the eggs with her movements. It is impossible to heat the egg evenly even if you have a fan type incubator that heats up the interior of the egg quite evenly.

- The next thing to keep in mind is the transfer from the nest box to the incubator. Line a container with wood shavings and place the eggs away from each other. Even the slightest bump can crack an egg. You need to know that a cracked egg has very few chances of hatching.

- The incubator will also have a humidifier that will maintain the moisture levels inside the incubator. The temperature and the humidity should be set as per the readings advised for Amazon Parrots. That is the ideal condition for the eggs to hatch.

- In case you want to be doubly sure, you can also check the temperature with a mercury thermometer regularly.

- It is safest to place the eggs on the side when you put them in the incubator. They are stable and will not have any damage or accidents.

- Heating the eggs evenly is the most important thing when it comes to the chances of hatching the egg. Make sure you turn the eggs every two hours over 16 hours. This should be done an odd number of times. The next step is to turn the eggs 180 degrees once every day.

- Keep a close watch on the eggs in the incubator. It is best that you get an incubator with a see through lid. This will let you observe and monitor the eggs. If you notice that one of them has cracked way before the incubation period ends, take it out of the incubator. If the eggs have a foul smelling discharge, begin to take an abnormal shape or change color, you need to remove them as they could be carrying diseases that will destroy the whole clutch.

- Usually, Amazon Parrot eggs will pip after 24-48 hours of completion of the incubation period.

- The hatching of the egg begins when the carbon dioxide levels in the egg increase. This starts the hatching process. All baby birds have an egg tooth which allows them to tear the inner membrane open. Then they continue to tear the egg shell to come out.

- The muscles of the chick twitch in order to strengthen them and to make sure that he is able to tear the egg shell out successfully.

- Never try to assist the hatching process unless you are a professional. If you feel like your chicks are unable to break out of the egg shell, you can call your vet immediately.

Watching the eggs hatch is a magical experience. You can do a few small things to make your clutch more successful. For instance, if you are buying a brand new incubator, turn on the recommended settings and keep it on for at least two weeks before you expect the eggs to be placed in them.

Make sure that the incubator is not disturbed. Keep all the wires tucked in to prevent someone from tripping on it and disturbing the set up or turning the incubator off. It is best to place this incubator in areas like the basement that are seldom used by you or your family members.

5. Caring for the chicks

The biggest challenge that you will face is deciding between letting the birds parent the young ones or hand raising them yourself. If you allow the former, the baby birds will develop better parenting instincts that will help breed them in the future. In case of the latter, you will have birds that are friendlier and more accepting towards humans.

Most Amazon Parrot owners take the mid-road and co-parent the birds. This is ideal as the baby birds get the best of both worlds.

Hand raising Amazon Parrots

If you decide to hand feed the baby birds, the ideal age to remove them from the cage is when they are about 3-4 weeks old. This is when the birds are in their pin feather stage. Their feathers look like quills at this stage.

This is the best age as the birds are able to hold the body heat and will not require any artificial heat. These birds also have the advantage of being raised by their parents and will be healthier. Immunity is better as the parents will pass on antibodies while feeding the babies.

Choose a formula recommended by your vet. Prepare the formula as per the instructions on the package. You need to make sure that the formula is heated to about 100 degrees F and not more than that. This can scald the insides of the delicate baby bird.

It is better to use a spoon to feed the baby as opposed to a syringe as you will be able to control the food going into the belly of the baby. That way you reduce the risk of choking the baby.

Feeding with a spoon is much slower. So chances of overfeeding are fewer. When the baby is full, you will be able to see the signs that will tell you when to stop feeding. You will also spend more time with the baby when you feed him with a spoon.

In case you pull the babies out of the nest earlier or have to hand feed them at an earlier stage because they were artificially incubated, you will have to purchase a brooder that will keep the babies warm as you feed them. The formula must be made very watery and should be given to the bird in small quantities. Then you wait for the crop to empty and feed the baby again. At a very young age, you may have to feed the baby every two hours.

In case of the pinfeather stage, you can feed the baby 4-5 times and give him some time to rest overnight. That way the crop will be fully empty and he will be ready for the next meal.

Co-parenting the baby birds

You may also choose to work with the Amazon Parrot parents and raise the chicks with them. This means that the Amazon Parrot parents will also be a part of the raising process. You will take turns between the feeding cycles and the babies will be removed from the nest to hand feed at least once a day.

Co-parenting is only possible when you have a very trusting relationship with your birds. If they can accept your attempts to take the babies out, then you can do this.

Your birds need to be extremely calm to allow you to co-parent the chicks. Otherwise they will develop aggressive behavior which they will direct at each other. The male may attack the female or they may even kill the hatchlings. You must back off if the birds show any signs of resistance.

However, if the birds accept your assistance, it can be a wonderfully rewarding experience for you. The responsibility is reduced on your part and on the part of the Amazon Parrot parents, the babies are more social and tame and the parents still have the pleasure of raising their own young.

It does not matter how you choose to raise the birds. Remember that all the experiences are equally rewarding. You may choose to add these birds to your flock. That is, however, not a practical thing to do as Amazon Parrots that have mated once will do so every year and the babies have a life span of about 30 years or more. So, it is a good idea to find these babies loving homes when they are a few years old.

Breeding Amazon Parrots is not for everyone. So make sure that you only do it if you are up for challenges such as the parents abandoning the babies within a few days of the eggs hatching.

In case you find the first experience with the chicks less exciting, you can discourage breeding by disallowing ideal nesting conditions as mentioned above. Some pet Amazon Parrot owners also avoid raising chicks because they find it very hard to give them away.

6. Weaning baby birds

You can wean a baby bird when he is about 4 weeks old. Weaning means to make the bird capable of eating his food without any assistance.

This will take some understanding and training for your baby bird. So you need to be as patient as possible.

Begin by leaving cubes of fresh fruit on the floor of the cage and let the bird inspect it. Since Amazon Parrots are curious by nature, they will peck at it and try to understand the new food.

They may just leave the food alone and walk away or may try to take a piece off. Let the bird explore and after one hour of providing fresh fruits and vegetables, the cage should be cleaned out to prevent chances of spoiling foods lying around the cage.

As the bird gets familiar with the new food, he will eat bits of it. Take a note of the types of fruits and vegetables that your bird seems to like and include them in the diet.

Soon, you will see that the bird will begin to lose interest in the formula as he will be full with the food that he has eaten by himself. You can even try to leave pellets and seeds in the water bowl. As the quantity of eating foods on their own increases, the need for assistance will decrease. That way you will have a bird who has been weaned correctly.

Chapter 8: Health Issues in Amazon Parrots

Parrots in general are prone to several health issues. The primary causes include poor sanitation, poor nutrition and a lack of proper mental stimulation.

As a parrot owner, it is important to be aware of the common health issues so that you can identify them in the earlier stages and find the necessary treatment options.

One of the greatest issues with parrots is that they tend to hide the symptoms of illnesses for a long time. This is a defense mechanism of most prey animals. Since the symptoms of illnesses make them vulnerable to predators, they try to keep them under cover. You need to make sure that you are observant and identify even the smallest change from normalcy.

This chapter helps you identify common health issues and even gives you details of these diseases to help you manage them more efficiently.

1. How to tell if your parrot is sick?

The earlier you catch the condition, the higher the chances are of your bird getting medical attention before the issue is permanent or irreversible. These are the signs you must watch out for:

- The beak develops spots or abnormalities. If the beak is dry and is peeling or has any discharge, it is an indication of health issues.

- The bird is bleeding.

- Breathing is very difficult and strained.

- The bird lets out sharp coughs.

- Drooling is a common sign of yeast infection.

- The eyes of the bird seem to be red, swollen or runny.

- The skin seems to be itchy or sore. The bird may have bald patches or abnormal falling of feathers even when it is not the molting season.

- The bird is plucking out his own feathers.

- The position of the head is abnormal. This may manifest in the form of circling of the head or twisting that seems unusual. The head may even twitch or shake in some cases.

- The head has wet feathers and seem soiled. This is a sign that the bird has been vomiting, especially if the wetness is restricted to the head.

- The joints of the bird seem to be swollen and the bird is less mobile or is hesitating to stand up.

- The legs seem weak or may even be paralyzed.

- The droppings have more urine or have an abnormal color or consistency.

- The bird experiences seizures from time to time.

- The vent or the cloaca of the bird is swollen or has some soreness around it.

- The crop or the abdomen of the bird is extremely swollen.

- There are lumps or tumors on the body.

- The bird seems to have lost his voice or the voice of the bird shows sudden changes.

- The wings are drooping.

- The bird shows sudden fluctuations in his weight.

- Vomiting is a common sign of illness. Regurgitation is a common behavior in parrots. When the bird regurgitates, the undigested food is thrown out. If there is not food particle in the expulsion, it might indicate vomiting.

- The bird is refusing to leave the floor of the cage.

- The bird seems to be lethargic and uninterested in the toys.

- Food consumption reduces drastically or increases significantly.

- The bird may consume excess water or may not drink water at all.

With these signs, you can be sure that your bird needs medical attention. When neglected, the issue will escalate, often leading to sudden death in the bird. The more you interact with your birds, the more likely you are to observe even the smallest drift from normalcy.

2. Looking for a good avian vet

Your avian vet will be your biggest support when it comes to raising your bird in a healthy way. You should find a vet who makes you feel comfortable and is willing to answer your queries at all times.

Convenience is one of the most important factors when it comes to looking for an avian vet. Make sure that you find one whom you can approach easily when you find any problems with your bird. They should also have adequate knowledge to help your bird. Amazon Parrots are exotic birds and you need an expert who knows their anatomy well.

Once you find the perfect avian vet, make sure that you have their contact details available with you and with anyone who is taking care of the bird such as your family, friends, pet sitters etc.

Here are some useful tips to ensure that your bird is in the right hands.

Avian vets have a degree in veterinary medicine but have dedicated a large portion of their practice to birds. Every country has an association that vets can register under to stay updated about this science. One such association is the Association of Avian Vets or AAV. You can find all the registered avian vets in your vicinity using their official website which is www.aav.org.

If you are unable to find a good avian vet on this website, you have the option of asking a regular vet for leads. You may also contact Amazon Parrot clubs in your city for more information.

When you are choosing an avian vet, here are a few things that you need to look for:

- Staff that are trained to handle birds. They will be comfortable around your birds and will know a little bit about the species as well.

- There should be an emergency facility linked with the clinic in case your bird needs immediate attention. It is best to look for a clinic that even has a pet hospital for in house patients.

- The vet should have mostly avian patients. If he is only seeing one or two birds in a day, he is most likely not an avian vet. Some of the avian vets also deal with exotic pets like reptiles but will dedicate most of their practice to birds.

- Each examination should be for at least 30 minutes. If the interval between each patient is just about 15 minutes, your bird may not be getting a thorough examination.

- The clinic should be as close to your home as possible. Drives are extremely stressful for pets and should be minimal.

Your avian vet should also be updated with the facilities available for birds. If he is part of the AAV or attends regular seminars about avian medicine, you can be sure that your bird is in great hands.

To be sure that you have chosen the right vet to treat your bird, here are a few questions that you should ask him or her upon your first visit:

- **How long have they been working with birds?** The more experience they have, the better qualified they are. You need to find someone who has a solid background to make sure that your beloved pet is in good hands.

- **Have you worked with Amazon Parrots before?** Although it may seem like all parrots are the same, each species has its own requirement and demands. The more your vet has worked with the species of parrot that you have, the more experience they will have.

- **Are you part of the AAV?** While it doesn't mean that a vet who is not part of this organization is not qualified enough, someone who is part of it is definitely a lot more reassuring. You see, the AAV only promotes highest quality medical healthcare for birds and ensures that all its members are updated.

- **Do you have birds at home?** It is certainly an advantage if your vet is a bird owner. That will give him a lot of hands on experience with the body language of the bird which will help make treatment sessions less stressful.

- **Is there an after-hours facility or emergency facility?** An accident does not occur with warning. So you need a vet who can be available or make some medical assistance available to your bird should some such incident occur.

- **What are your fees?** This is definitely a question you should ask, even if you feel awkward about it. If you are unable to afford the veterinary charges of a certain vet, you can look for more options. Every vet will have a fee schedule chart that will tell you what exactly you can expect when you sign up for a service.

- **Are house calls an option?** In some cases, the bird may be too severely injured or unwell to take him to the vet. Then, it will become necessary for the vet to come to you.

- **How many examinations are recommended per year?** Usually, a vet will recommend about one thorough examination per year. This is done to make sure that your bird is always in good health.

A qualified avian vet will answer all your questions patiently and without any hesitation. The manner in which they respond to questions will also tell you if their personality is compatible to you or not. This goes a long way in building a good relationship with your vet.

Locating your avian vet

The most difficult part about having a pet bird is locating a qualified avian vet. There are a few resources that you can try to find good leads:

- The yellow pages is the best way to start. This will have a list of specialized vets along with their qualifications.

- The official website of the Association of Avian vets will list a number of qualified avian vets who will be able to care for your bird.

- You can contact the veterinary medical association in your state for information.

- Speak to other bird owners and look for reliable vets in your vicinity.

The closer your vet is to your home, the easier it will be to take your bird for a checkup. Additionally, a vet who is located nearby will be able to deal with emergencies more effectively.

3. Bacterial diseases in Amazon Parrots

It is very common for birds to develop bacterial diseases. Most often inappropriate husbandry is responsible for making the birds develop these conditions. Improper nutrition leads to compromised immunity that makes the birds more susceptible to these infections.

Juvenile birds and neonates are even more susceptible to these conditions. The respiratory tract and the gastrointestinal tract are the first ones to get affected by these bacteria.

There are various strains of bacteria that affect birds out of which strep, staph, citobacter and E.coli are the most common ones. These are the bacteria that are associated with humid areas, dust, old food, seed, grit and water. In some birds, natural resistance to these bacteria may be compromised due to reproductive diseases in the parent.

Most common symptoms of bacterial infection

- Droppings that are watery and green in color.
- Sneezing
- Rubbing the eyes incessantly
- Swallowing constantly
- Coughing
- Yawning
- Coughing
- Change in voice or loss of voice

Bacterial infections, caused by either ingestion or inhalation, are life threatening if left unattended. The exact type of bacteria needs to be identified before giving the bird any form of treatment. That it is when you can treat it perfectly and also prevent it from recurring.

Treatment and precautions for common bacterial diseases

- Antibiotics are administered after the culture test is complete.

- Antibiotic drops are given directly to the bird if he is very ill. You can even inject the antibiotics in these cases.

- If the infection is mild, you can administer the antibiotics through drinking water. You need to make sure that the bird is drinking water when you take this approach.

- All the seed, fruit and grit should be removed from the cage.

- Disinfecting the cage on a regular basis is a must.

- The seeds that you provide must be sterile.

- The bird must never be left out of the cage unsupervised.

- If your bird has not recovered fully, you need to make sure that you do not allow him to wander around the house.

There are several things that you can do in order to accelerate recovery in your bird. You can give the birds Turbo-boosters and also energy supplements.

Special Fvite with sterile seeds can be included as a part of the diet of your bird.

Once your antibiotic treatment is complete, you can give your bird loford and dufoplus in water. You need to make sure that your bird is eating and drinking well. If he is not doing so, your vet may have to force feed him.

Bacterial infections can become very severe in the long run. They will damage the kidney and liver if ignored and the bird becomes susceptible to a lot of illnesses in the future.

It is the responsibility of the owner to understand how a certain disease originated in order to help the bird recover faster. In order to ensure that your bird does not have repetitive episodes of infection you can get a complete health program from your vet and follow it till your bird is fully recovered.

Paying attention to bacterial infections is very important as humans can also be affected by certain strains of bacteria. The droppings of the bird can spread bacteria. Children are especially susceptible to infection and must be kept away from a sick bird. One example of a bacterial strain that affects Amazon Parrots and humans is campylobacter.

Remember that bacterial infections are usually related to the surroundings of the bird. If there is any contamination that enters the mouth of the bird, it will lead to the disorder.

Of course, even the best kept birds may be susceptible to infections. If this happens, it becomes even more important for you to make sure that you understand the source of the infection and try your best to prevent any more in the future.

Here are a few strains of bacteria and the common sources of infection for each one of them.

E.coli
- Fluctuation of temperature
- Draught
- Stress
- Contaminated food or old fruit
- Wet areas
- Dirty cages

Strep
- Underlying viral infection
- Cold stress
- Dust
- Poor quality of food
- Stress

Staph
- Mice
- Dust
- Poor seed quality
- Contamination in the air conditioning

Diplococcus
- Stress
- Mice

Citobacter and Pseudomonas
- Poor water conditions
- Poor cage hygiene

Many owners believe in a holistic approach to prevent these infections. You may also try the following after consultation with your vet.

- **Goldensea:** This herb is used for its strong antibiotic property. It is effective against E.coli, staph and strep.

- **Echinacea:** This herb is known for killing several pathogens that cause diseases including protozoa, fungi and bacteria.

- **Licorice root:** This herb is antiviral and antibacterial in nature and is known to be effective against the most powerful strain of bacteria.

Most common bacterial conditions in Amazon parrots

In the case of Amazon Parrots, there are two conditions that you need to be extra cautious about. These birds are genetically predisposed to these conditions and may even be carriers of the condition in some cases.

Chlamydiosis

This is a condition that affects almost all companion birds. It is best that you follow all the federal regulations with respect to testing and quarantining for this condition if you plan to have an aviary or if you plan to breed Amazon Parrots.

This condition is caused by a type of bacteria called *chlamydia psittaci.* The incubation period of this strain ranges from 3 days to a couple of weeks.

The only concern with this condition is that it is easily transmitted from one bird to another through the feces. The bacteria stays infectious in debris that is organic for more than one month.

Symptoms in birds that are carriers:
- Anorexia
- Nasal and ocular discharge
- Dehydration
- Excessive droppings
- Lack of appetite
- Diarrhea

Symptoms in birds that are clinically ill:
- All of the above
- Monoystosis
- Leukocystosis
- Increase in bile acid level

Diagnosis

Diagnosis of this condition is quite difficult as the clinical signs are usually mild or absent. The most common methods of diagnosis include:

- Antigen and antibody tests
- Serological tests
- PCR testing
- Cloacal swab analysis

Multiple diagnosis methods must be applied because of the nature of this condition which is actually quite hard to identify and understand.

Treatments

- Doxycycline is the most common treatment option.
- Dietary calcium must be reduced during this treatment phase.
- Medicated feed may be administered if the condition is too severe.

You need to make sure that you devise a proper treatment plan for this condition as it can be transmitted to people quite easily.

Avian mycobacterosis

This condition is usually caused by different types of bacteria including *Mycobacterium avium, M.intercellulare, M.bovis, M.genovense and M.tuberculosis.*

This condition is progressive and usually affects the gastrointestinal tract of the bird as well as the liver. This condition is hard to diagnose because of the limited number of clinical signs available in the initial stages of infection.

Symptoms of Avian mycobacteriosis

- Weight loss
- Anorexia
- Diarrhea
- Depression

Diagnosis of the condition

- Acid fast staining of the culture
- Biopsy of the intestines, liver and spleen
- PCR testing
- Ultrasound

The difficult part in diagnosis is the fact that these strains of bacteria are very hard to culture. Therefore, if the culture test is negative it is not conclusive that the condition does not exist.

The other tests are not as sensitive. The best option is PCR testing of a sample of the bird's feces. In some cases, radiographs have been useful in determining the condition.

If you have an aviary with multiple birds, it is also hard to determine which of the birds is actually infected. If you are able to point out the birds that have the highest risk of being infected, you need to make sure that they are isolated and properly monitored.

Treatment
- Antibiotic treatment for 1 year or more
- Administration of multiple antibiotics
- Examination of your own husbandry practices

If your bird is in the advanced stage of this condition, it is less likely that he or she will be able survive. Although there have been no records of the conditions being passed on from birds to humans, you need to make sure that you take all the necessary precautions.

4. Viral diseases in Amazon Parrots
Viral infections in birds can be fatal. Making sure that your birds are checked by a vet on a regular basis is the key to keeping birds away from these diseases. With most viral diseases, the incubation period is very short and the birds may succumb to the infection overnight.

Here are some of the avian viral diseases that may affect Amazon Parrots:

Avian polyomavirus

This condition usually affects birds that are young. Usually adult birds are immune and in case of any infection, will shed the virus in just 90 days. Incubation period for avian polyomavirus is 10 days.

Symptoms of avian polyomavirus infection

In the most typical cases, a healthy juvenile bird that is still not a fledgling will develop crop stasis, lethargy and will die in just 48 hours of the onset of the condition. In rare cases, the following symptoms are recorded:

- Abdominal distention

- Cutaneous hemorrhage
- Feather abnormality

Diagnosis of the condition
- Examination of the cloacal swab
- Blood tests
- Virus neutralizing tests
- Antibody tests
- Necropsy testing of the chicks that have succumbed to the condition.

Prevention of the condition
- Keeping the aviary free from visitors.
- Making sure that new birds are only included in the aviary after 90 days of strict quarantining.
- Making sure that you keep up all the practices of hygiene.
- Stopping breeding for at least six months if the condition is diagnosed in any bird in the aviary.
- Disinfection of the nesting boxes and the aviary.
- Avoid purchasing birds from different sources.
- Avoid purchasing birds that have still not been weaned.

Treatment of the condition
As discussed before, avian polyomavirus has a very short incubation period and the symptoms are rarely seen before the bird succumbs to the infection.

You can opt for a vaccine that is available for younger birds. Making sure that you give birds that are breeding a dose of these vaccines at intervals of two weeks in the off season is a must.

You must also provide these vaccines to neonates before they are 35 days old. You have the option of a booster shot after about 3 weeks as well. Getting your birds this shot prevents the risk of infection to a large extent.

In general, there is no cure for this condition except preventive measures and supportive care after the condition has been diagnosed.

Gouldian Amazon Parrot Herpesvirus
This is a rather uncharacterized strain of virus that is known to affect Amazon Parrots, Crimson Amazon Parrots and Red faced waxbills. If you have an aviary with multiple birds, you will observe lesions in birds that

are affected. However, some of them may be completely unaffected by the virus.

Symptoms of Amazon Parrot Herpesvirus
- Listlessness
- Ruffled plumes
- Heavy breathing
- Nasal discharge
- Swelling in the eyelids
- Crusts in the cleft of the eyelid
- Inability to eat

After about 5-10 days of the first signs and symptoms of this viral infection, it has been observed that birds are unable to survive. Post necropsy, it was observed that the birds showed thickening of the fibnoid and discharge in the eyes and nostrils. Besides that, the internal organs seemed normal on all occasions.

Herpes virus are considered an alpha strain of virus because of which the incubation period is very short and the damage caused is quite serious. There is no cure for these conditions. All you can do is take preventive measures to make sure that the birds are quarantined properly, given ample food and clean water and are kept in the most hygienic conditions possible.

Avian bornavirus
Infections by avian bornavirus in birds were observed quite recently in birds with the first ever records being made in the 1970s. Since then, several species have been considered susceptible to the condition including Amazon Parrots. The first evidence of this condition affecting Amazon Parrots was observed in Estrildid Amazon Parrots.

This condition is progressive in a few cases or may develop overnight in others. Mortality rates are high in birds that have been affected by this strain of virus.

After several crop biopsies, it was discovered that affected birds have lesions in the heart, the gastrointestinal tract, the brain, spinal cord, lungs and kidneys. The disease may either be transmitted orally or through the feces. It is highly contagious and can be even more problematic if you have a mixed aviary.

Symptoms of avian bornavirus infections
- Chronic weight loss
- Increase in appetite followed by excretion of undigested food
- Regurgitation
- Convulsions
- Weakness
- Tremors
- Ataxia or inability to control movements
- Blindness

Diagnosis
- Biopsy of cloacal swabs
- PCR testing

These tests need to be carried out once every week for three straight weeks to determine if the bird is really infected or not. The virus is shed intermittently which makes it even more necessary for you to have multiple tests as well as differential diagnosis for conditions like toxicosis and foreign body obstruction before the conclusions are derived for infection by the avian bornavirus.

Treatment
- Providing the bird with food that is easy to digest
- Administering medications like celecoxib and meloxicam
- Isolation of infected birds as a method of disease prevention
- Regular PCR tests
- Good hygiene
- Ultraviolet light setting

Poxvirus infection
This is a large DNA virus that usually affects the respiratory tract, the oral cavity and the epithelial cells of the internal organs. It is believed that all birds are susceptible to this condition. In the case of aviary birds or companion birds, this condition can be avoided, as the birds will not be exposed to this virus if proper husbandry practices are followed.

This disease usually affects parrots and lovebirds. In the case of Amazon Parrots, your bird may only be a carrier and may never develop symptoms. However, for those with a mixed aviary, this is also cause for great concern as the disease spreads rapidly.

The infection may be cutaneous or systemic depending upon the strain of virus that has affected your bird, the age of your bird, the health of the bird and the route of exposure.

In the cutaneous form, you will notice that there are wart like growths on parts of the body that are unfeathered, including the area around the eyes and nares, the legs and the beak. Another form, which is the diptheric form, shows similar formations on the larynx, pharynx, tongue and the mucosa. The systemic form is differentiated by the characteristic ruffled appearance of the bird.

Symptoms of poxvirus infection
- Lesions on the eye, ear and oral cavity
- Lethargy
- Troubled or labored breathing
- Difficulty in swallowing
- Partial blindness
- Weight loss
- Skin lesions
- Ruffled appearance

Treatment of poxvirus infection
- Supportive care
- Fluids included in the diet
- Vitamin A supplementation
- Cleaning of the lesions on a daily basis
- Antibiotics
- Ointments for secondary infections
- Assisted feeding
- Mosquito control
- Indoor housing

It is also possible to provide your Amazon Parrots with certain vaccinations that will make them immune to certain strains of pox virus.

Avian influenza
Commonly known as bird flu, this is a condition that affects almost all species of birds. Most of the causal strains of virus do not affect human beings. However, it was recently discovered that some strains, like the A(H7N9), cause serious infections in humans as well.

This is a condition that commonly affects waterfowl but can even lead to outbreaks on a large scale in an aviary set up. The virus is so potent that it has the ability to even affect other mammals. So, if you have other pets at home, you have to be very careful and watchful.

This disease has a very aggressive progression. This means that the disease can spread within a few hours and can lead to death as well.

Symptoms of avian influenza
- High fever
- Diarrhea
- Vomiting
- Coughing
- Abdominal distension
- Decreased egg production
- Inflammation of the trachea
- Congestion
- Hemorrhage
- Edema
- Lack of limb coordination
- Paralysis
- Blood in the nasal and oral discharge
- Greenish color of the droppings

Treatment
- Vaccination is the best option to prevent the disease altogether

This condition can be serious if the strain of virus that affects the bird affects humans as well. In many states it is a mandate to report the outbreak of avian influenza in your aviary to a regulatory authority. Your avian vet should be able to help you with this.

In most cases, antiviral compounds cannot be administered to the bird unless it is approved by these regulatory authorities. Even the vaccination that is used on your birds needs to be approved by the USDA or by the state veterinarian.

5. Parasitic diseases in Amazon Parrots

There are both endo and ectoparasites that can affect Amazon Parrots. These parasites are mostly found in unhygienic conditions. While they are not always fatal, there are chances that the symptoms only become obvious when the bird is already very unwell. That is the only reason why parasitic infections are a threat to the bird's life. In most cases, a bird seems completely normal and the symptoms become severe overnight.

Here are a few parasitic infections that Amazon Parrots are most susceptible to:

Coccidiosis

This condition is caused by a certain parasite that is usually found in the intestinal tract of birds. The disease is transmissible and is passed on through the feces or through interaction. The condition is highly contagious and you will notice several birds being infected immediately after you notice the first case in your aviary.

Symptoms of coccidiosis
- The vent area is wet
- The bird has consistent diarrhea
- The feathers are fluffed up
- The bird has very little energy when you approach him
- The bird tends to sleep a lot

Treatment
- A course of sulfonamide or sulphadim is required
- The cage needs to be cleaned regularly to prevent any sort of infestation in your aviary.
- The drinking containers should be made only from glass or plastic while providing any antibiotics
- You may continue a course of broad spectrum antibiotics.

Parasitic worms
If your bird is being fed any live foods, worms are easily picked up. It is therefore necessary for you to make sure that the live food that you give your bird is fresh.

Another source of parasitic worms is the droppings of birds in the aviary. If the parent bird is a carrier of parasites, they may transfer it to the young while feeding.

When you have an outdoor cage, you need to make sure that there are no droppings of wild birds in your aviary. This is the primary source of several parasites and infectious diseases.

Symptoms of parasitical worms

- Weakness
- Worms are spotted in the feces of birds
- Worms are seen in the water dishes

The disease is fatal only when the condition is not treated properly. The most common worms that affect Amazon Parrots are threadworms, caecal worms, tapeworms, gapeworms, tapeworms and roundworms.

Treatment:
- Have a routine worm management program for your bird
- A broad spectrum wormer like levamisole can be administered to the bird
- Have your birds tested regularly

Scaly face

This is a condition that is also known as Knemidocoptes jamaiscensis. When mites borrow into the feathers of the bird and lay eggs there, this condition is caused.

The condition gets worse when the eggs that have been laid in the feathers actually hatch. The most common way of transmission for this condition is when the parent birds feed the young. It has been observed in adult birds as well but the source of transmission is not very well known.

Symptoms of scaly face
- A scaly film is seen on the skin
- The scales may be formed on the eyes if left untreated
- Scales are seen on the legs of the bird

If you ignore this condition it will become fatal as the scales will slowly spread all over the body. The parasites are demanding and will lead to the death of the host.

Treatment
- Paraffin is administered to birds that have been affected by this condition.

Air sac mites

This is one of the most common conditions that you will see in Amazon Parrots. The mite that causes this condition is scientifically called *Sternostoma tracheacolum.*

The condition affects the respiratory system of your bird, leading to a lot of labored breathing. The disease is transmitted during courtship and also when the parents feed their young.

Symptoms of air sac mites
- Coughing
- Loss of voice
- Abnormal chirping
- Labored breathing
- Fatigue

Treatment
- An insecticide is used to eradicate the mites fully.
- A spray containing ivermectin can be used in the cage.
- All birds, including the ones that are not affected should be treated for air sac mites.

These parasites have a life cycle of 6 days before which you need to make sure that your bird is treated. If the eggs hatch before treatment, the process becomes a lot more tedious and the condition progresses rapidly.

6. Nutritional deficiencies

Obesity

This condition is prevalent in many pet parrots. They are given a diet of high fat nuts, seeds and even table scraps. In some cases, overfeeding and not providing the bird with enough exercise will lead to obesity.

When a bird is about 20% more than the ideal weight, it is said to be obese. The weight of the bird's body will lead to lameness while he may experience respiratory issues if the concentration of the weight is in the abdominal area.

If your bird is diagnosed with obesity, it is a good idea to change the diet to a pelleted one with adequate portion control. Encourage your bird to exercise by keeping several food bowls around the cage to encourage him to walk around. Climbing and balancing toys also improve the physical activity of your bird.

Vitamin A deficiency

Vitamin A is one of the most important nutrients in a bird's diet, as it affects the immune system. Seed diets that contain even 50% seed and 50% pellet lead to vitamin a deficiency or hypovitaminosis A.

The symptoms of vitamin A deficiency include:

- Sneezing
- Nasal discharge
- Periorbital swelling
- Conjunctivitis
- Dyspnea
- Excessive urination
- Excessive water consumption
- Blunt or absent papilla
- Anorexia
- Development of white plaques in the sinuses and eyes

The treatment process involves dealing with the secondary infections, if any, and supplementing the bird's diet with Vitamin A. You can add natural sources like spirolina in the food of the bird to get better results.

Iodine deficiency

Although this condition is not very prevalent with the fortified pet foods, you need to be aware that a deficiency of iodine can lead to goiter or thyroid hyperplasia.

The most common symptoms are:
- Wheezing
- Clicking
- Respiratory stidor

You can use Lugol's iodine until the signs of iodine deficiency have subsided or been removed completely.

Calcium, Vitamin D3, Phosphorous deficiency

Most seed based diets will lead to a deficiency in calcium, amino acids and phosphorous. These seeds are also quite high in their fat content.

Metabolic bone disease

If the bird has an imbalanced calcium to phosphorous ratio, there are chances that he will develop hyperthyroidism. This is most common in younger and old birds.

Along with a lack of calcium, most birds have to cope with a deficiency in Vitamin D3, as they are housed indoors without adequate access to sunlight.

In the case of younger birds, a lack of calcium in the diet will result in deformation and curvature in the longer bones as well as the vertebrae.

The common signs of metabolic bone disease are:
- Ataxia
- Seizures
- Deformation
- Repeated fractures
- Thin shelled eggs
- Decreased egg production and hatchability
- Death of the embryo
- Egg binding

The plasma calcium levels are studied to diagnose a possible deficiency in calcium levels. Supportive care, along with necessary vitamin D and calcium supplementation is the best option. It also a good idea to provide your birds with a full spectrum light if they do not have enough access to natural sunlight. In the case of recurring fractures, bandaging and cage rest is necessary with adequate doses of pain killers.

If you can provide your bird with an outdoor cage, it will allow them to get natural light in abundance. If your bird's wings have been clipped, they can be taken outdoors, provided you keep a close eye on them.

Vitamin D toxicosis

While excessive oral calcium does not cause any health issues in birds, if you give them too much oral vitamin D3, there could be an accumulation of calcium in the tissues of the body including the kidneys. Make sure that you provide supplements only after consulting the vet.

Iron storage disease

The condition of having excessive accumulation of iron in the liver is called iron storage disease. It is also called hemachromatosis. As the level of iron increases, the lysozomes in the liver get damaged and release ions that lead to damage by oxidization in the membranes of the organs. It also leads to an improper metabolism of proteins.

Iron storage disease is not very common in pet birds but they are constantly at risk if proper diet is not provided. If the intake of iron is too high, it leads to this condition. There are other factors like genetic predisposition and stress that can cause this condition. Even an increased vitamin C intake will lead to storage of iron in the body.

The most commonly affected organs are the heart, liver and spleen.

The signs of iron storage disease include:
- Weight loss
- Depression
- Distended abdomen.
- Dyspnea
- Circulatory failure

The condition can be diagnosed with a biopsy of the liver. Treatment normally includes modification of the diet and removal of iron from the body. You must provide the bird with a lot of fiber to prevent accumulation of iron in the liver.

Other nutritional concerns
- A bird may develop sensitivity to certain preservatives and dyes present in pellets.

- They may experience a failure in the right side of the heart if the diet consists mainly of seeds.

- Improperly stored food will lead to cirrhosis.

- Your bird may not be eating everything that you provide even if you are making the effort of giving them a balanced meal. This must be dealt with by providing adequate supplements.

- If you are adding supplements, make sure that the bird is observed properly. Usually, these supplements are not palatable and the bird may stop consuming water, leading to dehydration.

- Never give your bird any foods that contain caffeine, alcohol, salt, refined sugar or dairy products.

In the wild, Amazon Parrots spend most of their time foraging. In the case of pet birds, they have access to one food bowl that gives them their entire caloric intake. However, with less energy spent, they will develop nutritional issues. Make sure that your bird has a healthy lifestyle.

It is a must to provide your bird with toys and adequate mental stimulation. A large enough cage is the first step to helping your bird burn some energy if it has enough toys and stimulators.

7. Preventive measures against common diseases

There is no better way to keep your bird healthy than preventive care. Since most illnesses spread so fast in Amazon Parrots, it is best that you take all the precautionary steps possible to prevent this sort of infection in the first place. Here are some tips that will help you maintain the health of your little feathered companion:

- Make sure that the diet is wholesome and nutritious

- Clean the cage and its contents regularly

- Take your pet to the vet for an annual checkup without fail

- Any new bird that is introduced to your home must be quarantined without fail

- The bird must have a lot of clean water to drink

- Your bird must be mentally stimulated in order to ensure good health

- Spend enough time with your bird to prevent any behavioral problems

- You need to make sure that he gets ample sunlight. It is a good idea to take the bird outdoors provided he is harnessed or is protected by a cage.

- Your home must be bird proofed even before you bring the bird home.

- Grooming and cleaning the bird is necessary.

Always keep your vet's number handy and learn as much as you can about your Amazon Parrot's health. That way, communicating with the vet also becomes easier and you will be able to provide better care for your bird.

8. Can Amazon Parrots develop behavioral issues

If you do not provide your bird with adequate mental stimulation, there is a chance that they develop issues such as biting and screaming. Here are some tips on dealing with the most common behavioral issues in Amazon Parrots.

Chewing

While chewing is a natural behavior for birds, it can become a problem when chewing is directed at your valuable belongings. In the wild, an Amazon Parrot will chew on branches and twigs to make his nest or home "customized".

Chewing is also very important for the bird to maintain his beak and keep it sharp. But, when it is not supervised and directed correctly, chewing can even become hazardous. For instance, a bird can chew on electric wires and get electrocuted or even start an electrical fire.

It is necessary for you to "parrot proof" your home to make it safe for the bird and also to keep your valuables out of the way. You can bring your bird several toys that they are allowed to chew on. This includes cuttlebones, branches, hard toys and lots more. Keep rotating these toys over the weeks to ensure that your bird remains interested in them.

Also make sure that your bird is always supervised when he is out of the cage. There is always a chance of accidents when you fail to do so.

Biting

The manner in which you approach your bird is very important. If you have any feelings of stress, anxiety or nervousness, your bird will catch on it immediately. Any apprehension when you approach the bird leads to a defensive bite. Remember, birds don't think much, they react to the stimulus that they get.

Another common cause for biting is using your hands to punish the bird. If you shoo the bird with a sharp wave or perhaps toss things at the bird, a negative association is created immediately.

What you can do is help your bird associate the hand with positive things. Hand feeding or giving the bird treats with your hand tells them that they have nothing to worry about when you approach them.

Lastly, territorial behavior makes the bird nippy. This happens especially when they are nesting or in their breeding season. Females tend to be more hormonal and territorial.

There are some things that you can do when the bird bites in order to correct the behavior:

- When the bird is about to bite, blow on his face gently to distract him.

- If your bird is perched on your arm when he is about to bite, just drop your hand by a few inches. This will put the bird out of balance. And any bird hates an unsteady perch. He will immediately learn that biting makes him lose balance.

- Just put the bird down on the floor if he bites. They are not happy being on the ground as it makes them feel vulnerable and will immediately distract them.

The one thing that you should never do is scream or shout at the bird. This is a response to the bird's behavior and that is precisely what he is looking for.

Training your bird to step up and to make him associate your hands with positive things is a sure shot way of keeping your bird's biting behavior at bay.

Screaming

Vocalizing at a certain time of the day, particularly at dawn and dusk, is common for Amazon Parrots. The only time you have an issue is when the screaming is a result of your going away from your bird or the bird not getting his way.

The best way to prevent screaming in Amazon Parrots is to make sure that you ignore the bird completely. That means, you must not even look at the bird. Yelling at the bird and asking him to stop only reinforces the behavior.

Then, reward the bird when he behaves appropriately. For example, if the bird begins to scream when you leave the room, let him do so. The moment he stops screaming and you can count up to 5 or 10, reward him.

You can also look for specific triggers that are making your bird scream. If it is something that threatens the bird, for instance a large bright object, just get it out of his sight to calm him down.

Ignoring the screaming bird is a habit that everyone in your family must practice. You need to make sure that no one responds to the bird with any sound or eye contact.

Redirecting your bird with foraging toys before you leave the room is one way of calming him down when screaming is associated with separation anxiety.

Phobia or anxiety

The first thing that you need to understand is the difference between phobia and fear. Fear is a good thing as long as it is rational. This includes your bird being wary of new people, new toys or a new environment. This can be reversed by familiarizing the bird with the change.

On the other hand, phobia is the excessive and irrational need to get away from a particular situation, object or person. You know that your bird is phobic when he will do anything he can to get away from his object of terror. This includes:

- Running in place
- Pushing his head through the cage bars, sometimes till he bleeds
- Crashing into walls violently
- Resisting strongly
- Aggressive response such as biting
- Throwing himself on the back to appear dead
- Fear of coming out of the cage
- Self-mutilation
- Feather plucking

You will mostly find phobias in birds that have been rescued from long term abuse and neglect. Improper breeding practices that do not allow the babies to develop properly can also lead to phobias. If the bird is force-weaned, the emotional development of the bird is stunted, leading to irrational fears.

There are several other factors such as a lack of socialization, being separated from other chicks in the flock too early, clipping the wings improperly or any traumatic injury or accident will lead to phobia in your bird.

That said, some birds are also genetically predisposed to being more anxious. You can seek your vet's assistance to provide medication to your bird to calm him down and reduce anxiety if you notice that it is affecting the well-being of your bird.

Interacting with your bird and trying to gain his trust will also go a long way in helping him overcome his phobia and become more confident.

Feather plucking

If your bird suddenly begins to pluck his own feathers out in an agitated manner or over-preens himself to the extent that he mutilates his skin and feathers, then it means that he has developed the issue of feather plucking.

When your bird resorts to feather plucking, you will see several bald spots. In addition to that, you will find feathers on the floor of the cage, even when it is not molting season.

There are several reasons for feather plucking in Amazon Parrots including:

- **Malnutrition:** If the diet of the bird is deprived of minerals like zinc, calcium, selenium and manganese, the skin becomes irritable, leading to feather plucking.

- **Boredom:** When the cage is too small for the bird to move around or if he does not have enough activities to keep him mentally stimulated, feather plucking becomes a means to keep himself engaged.

- **Lack of natural light:** Sunlight is a source of vitamin D. If your bird is kept in a dark area for long hours, he will become very depressed. This manifests in the form of feather plucking.

- **Stress:** If your bird is unwell or if he is in an environment that makes him feel stressed, such as a pet lurking around the cage very often, then feather plucking will begin. There are some medicines and supplements that can help him overcome feather plucking associated with stress. Treating the primary health issue will also reduce feather plucking in your bird.

- **Loneliness:** Amazon Parrots are solitary birds in the wild. However, it does not mean that they do not need any companionship. Spending time with your bird or finding him a compatible cage mate can help solve feather plucking related to loneliness.

- **Pain:** With birds, pain is not a feeling that they are able to understand. They know that they are uncomfortable and will try to relieve themselves by plucking feathers off the area where the pain is concentrated. There are also health issues like Psittacosis and Aspergillosis that have been commonly associated with feather plucking in birds. Your bird may have ingested a foreign object that makes his crop irritable, leading to this behavioral issue.

- **Food allergies:** Sensitivity towards a certain type of food will lead to feather plucking. Changing the diet or the brand of food that you give your bird is an effective way to deal with feather plucking.

In addition to the above, hormonal imbalance, improper diet and toxicosis can also lead to feather plucking in birds. Since there are so many causes for this condition, it is best that you let your vet examine the bird first before you begin to treat your bird.

Once the primary causal factor is eliminated, there are several medicines that will help the feathers grow back. You can also spray the body with an aloe vera solution to make the skin less irritable and promote the growth of feathers.

9. Dealing with injuries

Here are some common accidents that your bird may encounter and the necessary measures you have to take:

- **Skin wounds:** If the bird has cuts or bruises on the skin, wash it gently with 3% hydrogen peroxide. You can use gauze, q-tips or cotton to clean the area. In case the skin wound is caused by a cat or dog bite, wash the area and rush the bird to a vet. In order to stop bleeding in the skin, you can use a styptic pencil or you can also use cornstarch.

- **Bleeding nail or beak:** Sometimes, the bird's beak or nail can get entangled in the wires used to hang toys. It could also get caught in the bars of the cage. Then, you need to apply pressure on the injured area, directly using a paper towel or cotton gauze. If that is not good enough, you can use a styptic pencil or cornstarch to control bleeding.

- **Broken blood feathers:** Bleeding in the broken blood feathers is profuse and can even be fatal if you do not curb bleeding immediately. Use a styptic pencil to clot blood and hold the area down with a gauze or clean tissue paper.

- **Burns:** If your bird suffers from burns due to a hot stove, hot water, steam or even hot utensils, you can relieve the pain by misting the feathers with cold water. If the leg or foot is burnt, just dip it in cold water. Make sure that the water is not too cold. It should be cold water from the tap, not the refrigerator. You can use an antibiotic cream. But make sure that it is not oil or grease based as the heat is retained by such creams. In case of acid burns due to cleaning agents or detergents, flood the area with lots of cold water to relieve the pain.

- **Heatstroke:** The best thing to do would be to put the bird in an air-conditioned room. If you do not use air conditioning in your home, you can use cold water to mist the feathers and then turn on a fan. If you are turning a fan on, make sure that the bird is in a cage. Then, give the bird water to drink. In case of extreme heat strokes, it might become necessary to drop water into the bird's mouth directly.

- **Broken bones or wings:** It is best that you do not handle a bird with broken bones. This may happen by flying into a window, predator attacks, getting caught between a door etc. In case of a broken wing, you can hold the wing close to the body and secure it before transferring the bird to a travel cage. You need to remove any perch or toy from the cage if you are transporting a bird with broken bones. Line the floor with a soft towel with no loops.

10. First aid kit for Amazon Parrots

In order to provide timely care for your bird in case of an emergency, you need to have an emergency kit ready at all times. Here are a few things that you must include in your first aid kit:

- A blood coagulant: This helps prevent any profuse bleeding. A styptic pencil is the best option. If that is not available, you may use cornstarch or even flour.

- Tweezers: The bandages that you use for your bird will be very small in size. Having a pair of tweezers makes it easier for you to handle them.

- Cotton swabs: Any time you need to clean up a wound, cotton swabs will come in very handy. If you do not have any, you can even use Q-tips.

- Gauze: You need gauze to clean and wrap cuts, bruises and even bites. Sometimes, it also helps secure broken wings or bones.

- Bandages: If you want to have bandages in your bird's first aid box, make sure that they are non-adhesive. Specialized bandages are available for birds in most pet stores.

- Syringe: You will need a syringe to wash small wounds or the eyes of the bird.

- Disinfectants: The best option is hydrogen peroxide as it removes any germs that might cause infections to your bird.

- Towel: An injured bird can get aggressive and irritated. So using a towel to handle him will make things a lot easier for you.

Keeping a first aid kit handy is important. Also make sure that you are checking the contents for cleanliness and hygiene. If you notice that the bandages are dirty or dusty, replace them immediately. If not, your bird may develop secondary infections that are harder to deal with than the actual injury itself.

11. Can birds be insured?

Amazon Parrots are extremely expensive birds. Healthcare, too, is quite an expensive affair. While insurance for birds is not really easy to obtain, there are some options available to pet owners.

Getting pet insurance for birds is not very easy. Most insurance companies will provide policies for cats and dogs, but rarely for birds. However, there are some reliable ones that will give you decent benefits. The most common things that are covered by popular pet insurance are:

- Veterinary charges: They will pay for certain diagnostic procedures like X-rays and even some consultation fees. Veterinarian costs will mostly include emergencies only. In case of birds like the Amazon Parrot that have long lives, there may be a limit on the cover offered annually that may go up to $1500 or £3000.

- Escape or Loss/ Death: If you lose your bird to theft or death, they may cover some amount of the market value of an exotic bird. Theft and Escape cover requires you to fulfill some security conditions such as purchasing a five lever lock for the cage door.

- Public Liability: This covers any damage cause by your bird to another person or property.

- Overseas covers: This is necessary for you to travel with your pet to some countries.

The cost of your insurance with all these covers will come up to about $150 or £280 a month. These covers are purchased separately and you can cut costs on things like overseas cover or public liability cover if you do not think that it is necessary. However, all these covers are highly recommended for all pet owners. You can compare the costs of various insurance plans online to find one that works for you. If you have multiple birds, some of them may also offer a 10% discount on the insurance cover.

The two most popular insurance plans for parrots are:

- Pet Assure: With this policy you can only have your bird checked by a vet in the network approved by them. If your vet is not part of this network, you need to find one that is or you will not be able to get the cover for vet costs.

- VPI: This insurance does allow you to see any preferred veterinarian. However, they do put a limit on the number of visits and the cover that they offer annually. So, you may not be able to get full coverage for any major procedure that your bird may have to undergo.

That said, there is no policy for birds that is perfect. So, if you want to choose the most reliable one it may be the one that your veterinarian is associated with. That way you can be assured of some cover at least. Make sure you put aside some savings each month to cover for emergency medical expenses for your Amazon Parrot.

Conclusion

Thank you for choosing this book. The information in this book has, hopefully, helped you realize what a special species the Amazon Parrot is. It can be one of the most delightful pets to have.

In addition to this, the goal of the book is to ensure that potential pet parents realize the responsibility of bringing one of these birds home. You can refer to this book as a guide to raising your bird. However, make sure that you load yourself with as much information as you can.

Interact with other pet parents, understand your own bird by spending time with him and read up as much as you can about this species.

Here is wishing you a great journey with your beautiful Amazon Parrot.

References

The more you learn about your bird, the better the care becomes. The Internet is one of the best places for you to learn about your Amazon Parrot. There are several reliable sources, such as bird forums where you can discuss your issues or queries with other Amazon Parrot owners and get practical tips. Here are some great websites and online sources for you to try out:

Note: at the time of printing, all the websites below were working. As the internet changes rapidly, some sites might no longer be live when you read this book. That is, of course, out of our control.

- www.beautyofbirds.com
- www.premiumparrots.com
- www.lafeber.com
- www.bagheera.com
- www.thegabrielfoundation.org
- www.peteducation.com
- www.animal-world.com
- www.petparrot.com
- www.parrotsecrets.com
- www.birdtricks.com
- www.au.answers.yahoo.com
- www.neotropical.birds.cornell.edu
- www.rioyou.blogspot.in
- www.avianadventuresaviary.com
- www.itis.gov
- www.blog.parrotessentials.co.uk
- www.gccmadcap.blogspot.com
- www.myconure.com
- www.forums.avianavenue.com
- www.caiquesite.com
- www.shadypines.com
- www.parrotforums.com
- www.city-data.com
- www.theparrotclub.co.uk
- www.parrotdebate.com
- www.community.parrot.com

- www.parrotislandinc.com
- www.parrotsinternational.org
- www.pets.thenest.com
- www.sciencedirect.com
- www.informationvine.com
- www.what-when-how.com
- www.upatsix.com
- www.animals.nationalgeographic.com
- www.tailfeathersnetwork.com
- www.parrotalert.com
- www.petful.com
- www.talkparrots.com
- www.northernparrots.com
- www.windycityparrot.com
- www.pbspettravel.co.uk
- www.companionparrots.org
- www.linkinghub.elsevier.com
- www.pets.thenest.com
- www.astepupbird.com/

Copyright and Trademarks: This publication is Copyrighted 2018 by Zoodoo Publishing. All products, publications, software and services mentioned and recommended in this publication are protected by trademarks. In such instance, all trademarks & copyright belong to the respective owners. All rights reserved. No part of this book may be reproduced or transferred in any form or by any means, graphic, electronic, or mechanical, including photocopying, recording, taping, or by any information storage retrieval system, without the written permission of the authors. Pictures used in this book are either royalty free pictures bought from stock-photo websites or have the source mentioned underneath the picture.

Disclaimer and Legal Notice: This product is not legal or medical advice and should not be interpreted in that manner. You need to do your own due-diligence to determine if the content of this product is right for you. The author and the affiliates of this product are not liable for any damages or losses associated with the content in this product. While every attempt has been made to verify the information shared in this publication, neither the author nor the affiliates assume any responsibility for errors, omissions or contrary interpretation of the subject matter herein. Any perceived slights to any specific person(s) or organization(s) are purely unintentional. We have no control over the nature, content and availability of the web sites listed in this book. The inclusion of any web site links does not necessarily imply a recommendation or endorse the views expressed within them. Zoodoo Publishing takes no responsibility for, and will not be liable for, the websites being temporarily unavailable or being removed from the Internet. The accuracy and completeness of information provided herein and opinions stated herein are not guaranteed or warranted to produce any particular results, and the advice and strategies, contained herein may not be suitable for every individual. The author shall not be liable for any loss incurred as a consequence of the use and application, directly or indirectly, of any information presented in this work. This publication is designed to provide information in regards to the subject matter covered. The information included in this book has been compiled to give an overview of the subject s and detail some of the symptoms, treatments etc. that are available to people with this condition. It is not intended to give medical advice. For a firm diagnosis of your condition, and for a treatment plan suitable for you, you should consult your doctor or consultant. The writer of this book and the publisher are not responsible for any damages or negative consequences following any of the treatments or methods highlighted in this book. Website links are for informational purposes and should not be seen as a personal endorsement; the same applies to the products detailed in this book. The reader should also be aware that although the web links included were correct at the time of writing, they may become out of date in the future.

Made in the USA
Middletown, DE
26 November 2021

53496174R00060